Praise for:

Now Hiring:
Criminal Justice Professionals
An Insider's Tips for Seizing the Ethical Edge

"While directed at individuals who desire to become criminal justice professionals, this powerfully superb and insightful book provides the utmost thorough guidance to persons thinking about entering any career field requiring complete honesty and unquestionable integrity."

—Senior Judge Arthur L. Burnett, Sr., National Executive Director
National African American Drug Policy Coalition, Inc.

"This book serves up a 'no holds barred' straight talk about real events and situations. If you are sincere about your decision to join the noble ranks of those committed to a career in criminal justice, you must read this book. In current-day terms, I am wowed."

—John McAuliffe, Chief of Police (Ret.), Eastern Michigan University
Past President, International Association of Campus Law Enforcement
Administrators

"Uncertain about pursuing a criminal justice career? Now Hiring: Criminal Justice Professionals can be an integral part of the decision. Dr. Rogers' focus on one's experiences— both past and present—and her concise emphasis on the in-depth and lengthy hiring process will better prepare those intending to enter the field of law enforcement."

—Gregory Shiffer, Police Officer

Now Hiring:
Criminal Justice Professionals
An Insider's Tips for Seizing the Ethical Edge

June Werdlow Rogers, Ph.D.

CABLE PUBLISHING

Brule, Wisconsin

Now Hiring: Criminal Justice Professionals
An Insider's Tips for Seizing the Ethical Edge

Second edition: Revised and re-titled from **Becoming Ethically Marketable**
A Guide for Criminal Justice Majors and Recruits

Published by: Cable Publishing
              14090 E Keinenen Rd
              Brule, Wisconsin 54820

              Website: www.cablepublishing.com
              Email: nan@cablepublishing.com

Reasonable efforts have been made to publish reliable data and information, but the author and publisher cannot assume responsibility for the validity of all materials or for the consequences of their use.

ISBN: 978-1-934980-53-8
       1-934980-53-6

Library of Congress number: 2011933977

Cover design: Larry Verkeyn – larry@lvmultimedia.com
Illustrations: Rayfield Rogers, Jr.

Printed in the United States of America

This book is dedicated to my God

and my beloved country,

the United States of America.

About the Author

Retired Special Agent in Charge June Werdlow Rogers, a former federal law enforcement executive with the U.S. Drug Enforcement Administration (DEA), received a Ph.D. in Criminal Justice and Criminology at the University of Maryland. Her expertise in the specialized field of narcotic law enforcement led her to conduct extensive research, prepare papers, make presentations, and prompt policy changes within her agency. Her doctoral dissertation, "A Descriptive Exploratory Analysis of Corrupt Drug Agents and their Careers in Corruption," formed the basis for several presentations and policy recommendations in the area of ethics.

After more than two decades with the DEA and evaluating criminal justice recruits, Dr. Rogers identified the need for criminal justice career aspirants to develop and maintain ethical behavior long before they seek employment in the field—and this inspired her to write *Becoming Ethically Marketable*, now revised and re-titled as *Now Hiring: Criminal Justice Professionals*. Her twenty-eight years of professional experience thoroughly inform the pages of this book. During her career, Dr. Rogers conducted successful investigations and served as an academy instructor as well as a first- and second-level supervisor before being elevated within the ranks of executive law enforcement. She retired in 2008 as the Special Agent in Charge of the New England Field Division. Her geographically diverse assignments took her to major U.S. cities including Baltimore, Detroit, Houston, New York and Boston, and additionally to the Virginia cities of Arlington and Quantico.

Dr. Rogers also served as a police officer with the Detroit Police Department and with Central Michigan University's Department of Public Safety. She has authored an acclaimed career women's leadership guide, *Cracking the Double Standard Code* (Cable Publishing, 2010), and contributed a chapter titled "Counseling Issues and Police Diversity" to *Police Psychology Into the 21st Century* (Martin I. Kurke and Ellen M. Scrivner, editors; Lawrence Erlbaum Associates, 1995). Additionally, she has been a speaker at the Academy of Criminal Justice Sciences' Conference, International Symposium on the Future of Law Enforcement, Federal Women in Law Enforcement Conference (WIFLE), and numerous other training seminars from entry to management levels. In 2011, Dr. Rogers delivered the commencement address to the graduates of Central Penn College. She continues to educate community groups in her areas of expertise.

During her tenure as a senior executive, Dr. Rogers received multiple performance awards for exceptional service. In addition to numerous awards and citations for her contributions to the field of law enforcement, she has been featured in print and online publications as well as on radio and television.

Now, Dr. Rogers is an Adjunct Instructor at Baker College in Allen Park, Michigan, where she instructs college students in criminal justice. She is married to Rayfield Rogers, Jr., and they make their home in a downriver community of Michigan's Lower Peninsula.

Comments for the author are welcomed and may be directed to her at her Web site: **www.urnotcrazy.com**

Contents

Part III—The Selection Process

Part IV—You Got It! Now Keep It!

Introduction

You're all set. You have finished school and earned that degree or certification. You've got your interview wardrobe at the ready. You are feeling great about your accomplishments and yourself, as you should, and now you're stoked to seek employment in your chosen field.

Everything will be well—as long as you are able to jump through the bigger hoop of being ethically marketable.

Perhaps with your earliest non-career jobs, it was simply a matter of filling out the application, going for an interview, and getting hired. It's not so simple in the field of criminal justice—or any field that requires a special level of trust between employer and employee. In determining if you are indeed qualified for a sensitive position, a hiring manager likely will launch an extensive background investigation. Unfortunately, in my experience it is clear that many applicants have not taken this very important aspect of the applicant screening process into consideration as they prepare for their careers. But it is essential that you take steps to ensure that your character will withstand the scrutiny of a thorough background check.

We are living in a time of declining personal values. Consider, for example, a survey of Americans in which 11 percent of respondents said it was okay to cheat a little on their tax returns and 5 percent said it was acceptable to cheat as much as possible—leaving 76 percent to declare that there should be no cheating at all. (Associated Press, 2002) Compare this to 1999, when 87 percent agreed that cheating on tax returns was unacceptable.

Even more startling and germane to our discussion is the evidence of cheating in recent years by criminal justice students. A poll undertaken by California State University criminology students to help determine whether Scott Peterson, accused in the death of his wife and unborn child, could be tried fairly in certain counties partly convinced a judge to order a change of venue for Peterson's trial. But then it came to light that some of the survey's results were fabricated. Subsequent probes resulted in a professor being discredited, suspended, and recommended for demotion. And almost half the class was charged with fabricating data and disciplined. (Turner, 2005) Most upsetting to the students' futures is that California State officials retained the documents with their admissions of cheating and could release them to prospective employers. (Mooney, 2004)

Erosion of values is problematic for law enforcement officials seeking qualified candidates for sensitive positions. It not only shrinks the pool of ideal applicants, but it may cause agencies to lower their hiring standards. For example, for certain jobs, some organizations have gone from zero tolerance for past drug use to forgiving "drug experimentation" in an applicant's background. This can become a slippery slope—as was seen with the Miami Police Department in the early 1980s, when recruits basically unsuited to be police officers were hired. The result was that by 1988 more than a third of those hired had been fired, with a notoriously dirty dozen known as the "Miami River Cops" convicted of serious crimes such as robbery, drug trafficking, and murder. (Delattre, 1989)

Commonly regarded as "rotten apples" by corruption researchers, such persons should be prevented from entering the criminal justice field. However, I do not believe that everyone who has made mistakes is necessarily crooked, as maturity and experience can change people for the better personally and professionally. The dilemma of every criminal justice administrator is that the science of identifying the truly rotten apples is inexact. Fear of the unknown may cause many administrators who find *any* questionable activity or behavior in a candidate's background to err on the side of caution and discount that candidate.

For those who do not protect their integrity and character, this hiring posture could constrain their potential to obtain a position in the criminal justice field. Rather than focus on the mundane aspects of job application mechanics, this book—through tips on passing the various screenings you will likely undergo—addresses how you can improve your chances for getting the job. These include an explanation of the important phases of the hiring process for the most sensitive criminal justice positions from the perspective of an employer seeking candidates with uncompromising integrity.

My own perspective is that of a criminal justice professional with 28 years of experience in the field. All of those years have been in law enforcement—providing me the basis for this overview of what I believe to be the most challenging of selection processes. The good news is that if you are able to withstand the scrutiny of the kind of background investigation many law enforcement officers face, you should have no problem making it through the hiring system of many criminal justice agencies, regardless of the position.

I practiced with three different law enforcement agencies in which I held a diversity of assignments, including executive management. These varied positions presented unique opportunities for outlooks and expectations of ethical behavior from coworkers, superiors, and the staff I was responsible for supervising, as well as from me. Although I have learned much over the years, I am still striving for perfection. Writing this book has re-illuminated many of my own poorer choices and caused me to cringe at times. Most of the decisions I wish I could forget occurred earlier in my career and were born of ignorance. I wish I had then, as you will find in these pages, a source of information and guidance.

I do not wish to come across as judgmental. But make no mistake: You *will* be judged on decisions made both prior to and during your criminal justice career.

Thankfully, as we mature, so usually does our decision-making and behavior. My primary goal is to help you identify ways to deal with your own decisions and determine the appropriate circumstances for public disclosure. When conducting the exercises herein, carefully consider which of your personal experiences are appropriate for discussion and which should remain mental exercises.

Pursuing a doctorate in criminal justice gave me the incentive to bridge the worlds of academia and practice. Although this work is not a research study, I view it as an opportunity to provide an informed yet common-sense guide that is useful to both practitioners and scholars. As you, the prospective criminal justice professional, read this book, I hope that either your resolve is strengthened in choosing this field based on your willingness and ability to continually build character that will contribute positively to it—or that you reach the realization that the ethical demands of this work are such that you have to seriously reconsider whether a criminal justice major (CRJ) is worth pursuing. Since your ability to enter the criminal justice field depends on your standard of conduct, it is important to know what is expected of you beforehand.

It has saddened me to see unfortunate situations where people have obtained the requisite degrees for a career in criminal justice only to find that previous conduct impeded their entry. This book emphasizes that it is just as important to prepare from a lifestyle standpoint as an academic one. Helping you to examine past choices and, by extension, assess your ability to obtain work as a criminal justice professional is a primary objective.

Wanted: Criminal Justice Professionals takes a practical, straightforward approach by using actual events to illustrate various points. To that end, life application exercises have been developed and are included throughout this book to assist you in analyzing your stance on various subjects—and to help you determine the extent your values and actions line up with the standards of the field. These exercises are designed to reinforce existing pertinent values and identify those that may need strengthening.

It is essential that you be honest with yourself while navigating these exercises. If you feel that you are unable to maintain honesty in a group discussion setting, perform the exercises in isolation. You do not necessarily need to write anything down, but you should emerge from a given exercise knowing your position and how it will make working in the criminal justice field either harder or easier for you.

A Chinese Proverb suggests that "a fool makes his own mistakes, but a wise man learns from the mistakes of others." Learn from the examples presented herein. Your willingness to do so can pay off by maximizing the likelihood that you will not unwittingly compromise your integrity—and miss out on that great criminal justice position you are working so hard to obtain.

Part I

Practitioners
in
Criminal Justice

Chapter 1

Why Work in the Criminal Justice Field?

Have you ever wondered how people who have really great jobs got them? Perhaps you have seen interviews wherein others have spoken of sacrifices made to obtain the experience and education required for appointment to impressive positions. Maybe they even had to take jobs paying substantially less as a stepping stone to get there. Less likely to have been discussed in these personal stories are the *character* requirements of the positions. Knowing the ethical demands of the criminal justice field can improve your chances of working in it.

Criminal justice is a broad field, with law enforcement being just one of many careers. There are high standards for hiring and ethical behavior among policing organizations, and since my own experiences originate from this field, examples from it will be cited heavily herein. If you strive to maintain the ethical standards of law enforcement, you will likely meet the ethical requirements of other criminal justice professions.

Your motivation for entering the criminal justice field will determine your difficulty in meeting its ethical standards. For this reason, I recommend that you make a self-evaluation—examining the reasons drawing you to this line of work. You have probably already heard that, as a general rule, criminal justice is not a lucrative profession. Like everyone else, criminal justice professionals need to earn a living so that they can take care of their families and their own needs; however, public service does not usually offer positions with compensation equal to that of jobs in other lines of work requiring similarly focused skills and character integrity. In making your career assessment, it is possible that you will rule out criminal justice as a profession because salaries tend to be lower in public service occupations compared to positions in the private sector.

You should not count on having the time or the opportunity to supplement your public service income by engaging in outside employment. Often, criminal justice professionals work well beyond the typical 9-to-5 schedule, and some governmental agencies—notably the Department of Justice—restrict their employees from engaging in extracurricular work, particularly if it conflicts with official duties.

This is not to say that you cannot make a comfortable salary in the criminal justice field. Rather, compared to other professional positions, you are not likely to become wealthy. With this in mind, if you have always wanted to earn a high salary or become rich, you may want to reconsider whether public service is the right career fit.[1]

If money is not the proper motivator for entering criminal justice, what is? Many with experience will say that they became public servants because they wanted to contribute to the betterment of society. As corny as that may sound, the desire to serve others is perhaps the noblest reason for going into public service. Still, though highly rewarding, at times the work in this field is taxing and thankless—so dedication is crucial.

---

[1] Or, you may wish to delay your entry into public service until after you have earned that "fortune." For example, I have seen lawyers work in the private sector and then become prosecutors or politicians—although I have witnessed more moving from the public sector to the private sector.

Chapter 2

What *Can* You Be?

Those aspiring to become criminal justice professionals probably have taken some initial steps. Perhaps in selecting your CRJ major, a survey or personality inventory helped you identify the positions that match your personal characteristics and traits. Additionally, your own reality check must include weighing the feasibility of whether you are likely to be able to obtain employment in the criminal justice field.

There are all sorts of limitations—including physical, intellectual, and economic—that can restrict a person's ability. In the criminal justice field, there is the additional constraint of a personal history that can impact job prospects. Delinquency research has led criminologists to embrace the maxim that "the best predictor for future behavior is past behavior." Human resource specialists embrace the past-future link to such an extent that conclusions are often drawn about future work performance based on past behavior as well.

You may also accept the premise that predictions can be made based on past behavior. Take a moment and think about someone you know well. Can you not frequently predict what they will do in a given situation based on how they have behaved in similar instances? For many of us, it is rare to be truly surprised by the conduct of people we are quite familiar with. And so it is that prospective employers, whether or not they are familiar with social science theories, will undoubtedly weigh heavily your past—including positive and negative behavior—as they consider your future.

Life Application Exercise #1

Recognizing that it is accepted in our society that what you have done in the past predicts what you are likely to do in the future, how well do you think you stack up? Based on what you know about yourself, do you believe that much of your past behavior suggests that you are a good risk or a bad risk for a criminal justice agency? Do you believe that the examples you used to gauge your risk are good predictors for how you will behave in the future with a prospective employer?

Based on past actions, do you feel comfortable and confident that you would be a good candidate? How competitive do you believe you are with other candidates based on just this factor alone? If the worst were known about you by an employer, would the selection committee still feel comfortable recommending your hire—especially if there were a lot of candidates and only a few jobs?

To a significant extent, you are the best judge of your past-future nexus because you have all the facts. You may feel that you are a good person, and even if you are aware of embarrassing conduct, you may not think that you are a poor risk. However, remember that you are not going to be viewed from your own perspective, but through the eyes of skilled criminal justice personnel whose goal is to match the right candidate to the right job. Recognizing that employers will look at your past should move you to commence viewing yourself from their angles. This, in turn, can help you decide if the criminal justice field truly is for you.

Commitment to a career in criminal justice is comparable to the commitment required by education. Beginning with a syllabus, a professor informs you of what is expected of you, and you in turn determine how much effort you are willing to put into getting the best grade you hope to receive. Then you decide whether to remain registered in that class, or whether to drop it and move on to something else. Perhaps you are not certain in the beginning, so you opt to give it a bit more time for consideration and possible crystallization. Try committing yourself to this book in a similar way to create a clear image of yourself and your ethical fitness.

Chapter 3

What Jobs?
Opportunities in the Criminal Justice System

Let's talk about the criminal justice system that serves as an extensive employer. Although at any given time some agencies are reorganizing and laying off workers, others are expanding and on the hunt for experienced help. Assuming that you are ethically marketable, let's consider the possibilities.

From police officers and sheriff deputies on the local level to troopers on the state level and agents and deputy marshals on the federal level, law enforcement agencies present a multitude of opportunities for sworn personnel. In addition, many law enforcement agencies employ other specialists and investigators, including forensic scientists, intelligence analysts and regulatory agents. The most recent census published by the Bureau of Justice Statistics (2007) indicates that there are about 1.1 million full-time state and local law enforcement employees in the U.S. Different federal agencies—such as the Drug Enforcement Administration, the Bureau of Alcohol, Tobacco, Firearms (ATF), and the U.S. Secret Service—have different areas of specialty and focus, and the types of crimes you will investigate and laws you will enforce depends on the agency for which you work.

Knowing how accused criminals navigate the criminal justice system can be useful in helping you identify additional job opportunities within the field. Once an individual is arrested and charged, the next contact is the courts. Typically there is a bail hearing to determine if the defendant will be released, and if so, what the conditions will be. This step in the process requires the services of a pre-trial service case worker, who makes recommendations concerning release conditions (e.g., drug treatment). If not released, the defendant will be remanded to the custody of a facility responsible for temporary lodging. This requires the services of jail guards and criminal justice professionals responsible for prisoner processing.

A judge may order that a defendant be released under certain conditions, pending a trial. The defendant may be monitored electronically or reside in a halfway house that may permit work-release periods. It is not uncommon for a conditional release to include supervision by probation officers and substance abuse counselors. Some of these pre-trial conditions are contracted out to the private sector but ultimately the branch of government through which the defendant is processed retains authority and responsibility. Even in jurisdictions where corrections and intermediate sanctions are contracted out, the employees who fulfill these services are still considered to be working within the criminal justice system and therefore are frequently held to high ethical standards through background checks.

At all levels of the process, there are court officers responsible for securing the courtroom and ensuring that the defendant remains in custody until released. (Federally, the U.S. Marshal's Service has this responsibility, while on the local level it is often the Sheriff's Office.) Criminal defense and prosecution lawyers, and of course judges, are principals in the process; the defendant and the governing body are represented by lawyers. Prosecuting attorneys[2] are generally regarded as part of the criminal justice system. Having legally established that there is enough evidence to demonstrate that a crime has been committed, the defendant is bound over for trail.

The next stage rests with an important decision from the defendant as a plea is entered, usually in consultation with a defense attorney. The prosecutor, who represents the interests of "the people," is involved at this stage if plea bargaining is entered into with the defense in order to obtain a guilty plea in exchange for a reduced sentence. A judge ultimately decides on acceptance of a plea as well as the extent to which the prosecution's recommendation will influence a sentence.

If there is a trial, there may be many hearings where motions are filed and the defendant may or may not be found guilty. If the defendant is found not guilty, the process stops; if an offender is convicted—either by pleading guilty or of a finding by a judge or jury—then there is sentencing. The trial and sentencing process represents many opportunities for paralegals and law clerks, who may be needed to research legal precedents and the criminal history of the defendant. Depending upon whether the

---

[2] While prosecuting attorneys are widely regarded as part of the criminal justice system, defense attorneys are not—a primary reason we will not focus on legal ethics. Lawyers have their own set of conduct codes, with much relating to bar regulations. I believe ethical standards for lawyers are less stringent than those of law enforcement staff because legal ethics appears more narrowly focused on the interests of clients versus society at large.

outcome is a prison sentence or an alternative punishment, other institutions of the criminal justice system can enter the picture.

From probation to incarceration, a host of sanctions are available to the judiciary. Alternative sentences such as boot camp and drug treatment programs encompass various professional positions relating to offender rehabilitation. Sentences which include incarceration require the services of correctional officers and some post-release offenders are monitored for a period of time by parole officers.

Processing through the United States criminal justice system can be lengthy and complex, and it may involve the services of numerous professionals. Additionally, there are some assignments[3] delegated to the private sector, such as electronic monitoring of offenders to assist governments. Where do you think you will fit in best?

Life Application Exercise #1

The hiring of correctional officers raises an interesting question about the appropriate age of candidates for certain criminal justice positions. Belluck (2001) reported that a correctional institution desperate for prison guards had lowered the minimum age from 21 to 19. Obviously, this adjustment was likely to increase the number of candidates, especially for positions not requiring a college degree. The same article pointed out that guards could expect to have a demanding job that included verbal abuse and feces being flung by inmates.

Are 19-year-olds generally mature enough for this line of work? Having started my own law enforcement career at age 19 in the Detroit Police Department (the minimum hiring age at the time was 18), I believe that it could be. The determining factor is the individual and his/her life experiences; even at age 30, some will never be mature enough, while others may indeed be ready before the end of their teens. Relevant questions for you, as a candidate, to ask yourself: How would you handle someone confronting or attacking you? Would it be your main intent to subdue the prisoner or would you really want to get a good fight on? In subduing an offender, are you likely to want to use the force necessary to neutralize a situation or would you want to dole out some extra punches for your personal satisfaction?

---

[3] These contract positions can present opportunities for CRJ majors to pre-enter the field. Often, contract employees are among those seeking permanent positions within various levels of government. Think of it as an audition: if your performance is regarded as exceptional, it can increase your chances for hire.

The U.S. criminal justice system employs many types of professionals. Your first big decision is to determine what you would like to do and identify which part of the system in which you wish to work. Is it in policing, corrections, probation, parole, or prosecution? To arrive at this decision, it is critical to identify the characteristics that will be useful to the criminal justice professional and his or her employer.

Part II

Deciding on and Preparing for a Career in Criminal Justice

Chapter 4
"Know Thyself"

Deciding whether criminal justice is the field for you can be quite involved. You must consider how your life may change, including the possible dissolution of friendships and cessation of certain activities. Can you keep a secret? Are you obsessed with money? Is working long hours for low pay objectionable? How are you on self-control? Are you easily tempted? You must ask yourself all these questions—and more—if you want to become a criminal justice professional.

Anyone approaching this field should know that it is easy to blow your chances well before you reach the gate. Be aware that no matter where you are with your schooling or chronological age, you are creating a character portrait with the decisions that you make. And at the point you begin to launch your career, that portrait will be analyzed and judged.

It is essential that you strive to make good decisions now to establish and bolster your integrity, because it only becomes harder as time passes. Deciding not to cheat is a good place to start. Cheating remains a real and growing problem in our society: According to the Josephson Institute, which examined the ethics of 12,000 high school students in 2002, 74 percent of student respondents admitted cheating on a test compared to 61 percent who acknowledged doing so in 1992. (Carlson, 2003)

Strength of character and a high degree of integrity are desirable among CRJ majors and criminal justice job candidates. With this in mind, know that anything that happens in your life involving law enforcement beginning at age 18[1] is likely to be available to criminal justice colleges and agencies evaluating your background.

---

[1] And possibly even earlier than age 18 if it involves being charged with a serious crime, such as murder, where prosecutors may charge one as an adult.

For example, are you aware that having a drug conviction can affect your ability even to obtain financial aid for college? Though the original law passed by Congress banning federal aid to college students with past convictions was modified; students who are convicted of a drug offense occurring during a period of enrollment are still affected.[2] But even if one does not depend on federal financial aid for college, having a drug conviction will adversely impact job prospects in the criminal justice field.

Another key question: How private is your "personal business?" Do you believe that conduct such as having heated arguments or fights with family members or drinking a few alcoholic beverages and then driving are your business and yours alone? The fact is that such behavior could result in your inability to get or keep a job in the criminal justice field.

While certain overt actions and activities are contrary to building a foundation for a criminal justice career, there also are less obvious things for which you can be held accountable. For example, are you aware that it is illegal to know about the commission of a felony and to fail to report it to the proper authority? This criminal inaction is known as "misprision of a felony"[3] and it carries a sentence of up to three years of confinement if proven. This statute has recently been enforced in drug cases to seize and forfeit the properties of landlords or business owners who knew drugs were being sold from these assets.

Avoid placing yourself in victimizing roles by persons who wish to minimize their risk of being detected as criminals. Drug traffickers and other predatory offenders frequently use front persons they believe police will not suspect to do their dirty work. Sometimes pawns are unaware they are being used. You may wonder how this is possible—but consider, for example, that a means by which drugs are smuggled into the country is in clothing. Items soaked in liquid forms of illegal narcotics make it easy for criminals to dupe the unsuspecting into becoming unwitting couriers. Still, aware or not, if you are the one "left holding the bag," you can be arrested and prosecuted.

Let's take a look at the U.S. Supreme Court ruling on a case titled Maryland v. Pringle.[4] According to Oyez (2003), the question presented to the court was this: If illegal material is found in a car and all passengers deny ownership, does the Fourth Amendment prohibition of unreasonable searches and seizures bar a police officer from arresting all the passengers? The court held that the arrest of Pringle, who was a passenger in the front seat of the car while the cocaine was found in the backseat, was legal. It ruled that there was probable cause to believe Pringle committed the

---

[2] Public Law 109-171.
[3] Title 18, USC, Section 4.
[4] Maryland v. Pringle (No. 02–809) was argued on November 3, 2003, and decided on December 15, 2003.

crime of possession of cocaine, either solely or jointly; and that the defendant's attempt to "characterize this as a guilt-by-association is unavailing." If you are arrested in this manner, getting a job in the field of criminal justice will be improbable.

Who Are You?

Knowing who you are can be very helpful in determining whether a criminal justice position is right for you. In an associate's observation of what was perceived as rigidity in my personality, it was suggested that perhaps I should seek another line of work so I could "lighten up." My response, since repeated on many occasions: "I am not who I am as a result of what I do, but rather I have chosen to do what I do as a result of who I am." This statement, over time, has served as a guide: It is important to select a career based on *who* you are, as opposed to what you are trying to make yourself. Even if you meet the basic qualifications of a job (e.g., age, degree, health, etc.), knowing who you are may help you avoid forcing a career fit.

One of those "who am I" qualities that I possess that I believe has been helpful in my work include a tendency to see the world more in terms of black and white than shades of gray. While everything is not necessarily defined in absolutes, many assumptions made in law enforcement are. For example, law enforcement officers must frequently interpret acts as legal or illegal, as misdemeanor or felony. Sometimes with misdemeanors, officers may exercise discretion as to whether an arrest will be made—but this estimation does not diminish the fact that the catalytic act was considered illegal. Such underlying black-and-white assuredness is a big plus in helping a law enforcement officer exercise his or her duties.

You are in the best position to examine yourself and identify exactly what you hold valuable—and this, in and of itself, is a value. This self-examination can focus on your likes and dislikes and comparatively can be used to determine the type of work best aligned with these and other personal qualities. But you must go beyond even this degree of inward scrutiny to find out if you can meet the ethical demands of a criminal justice position.

Life Application Exercise #1

How do you view the world—in black or white or shades of gray? Consider a controversial subject: the use of marijuana, an illegal drug, for medicinal purposes.[5] Do you think people should be arrested or prosecuted for using marijuana they claim alleviates pain and other symptoms if they do not possess the proper authorization or medical prescription? Do you see the issue as right, wrong, more right, more wrong, or are you in the middle of the road? Do you think your position on this issue could affect your ability to make an arrest or file charges if you were a law enforcement officer or a prosecutor?

Life Application Exercise #2

Knowing yourself is not restricted to conduct only; mental ruminations and pondering are also important. Dwelling on situations that you know are wrong can be problematic, especially if thought out to the point of making detailed plans. It is a slippery slope that can go from thinking: It would be nice to have $200,000 to thinking what specifically you would do with it, and then to fantasizing about shady undertakings (e.g., a swindle or scheme) that could result in such a windfall. Sometimes these thoughts, while not illegal in this form, can lead to steps that finally result in criminal action. Identify at least two things that you have been dwelling on: are they positive or negative?

---

[5] On December 16, 2003, the Ninth Circuit Court of Appeals ruled in favor of two people who possessed marijuana they claim was for medicinal purposes. This battle between the federal government and the State of California resulted in the decision that prosecuting medical marijuana users under the federal law is unconstitutional if the marijuana is not sold, transported across state lines, or used for non-medicinal purposes (Associated Press, 2003). The United States Supreme Court ruled in 2005 that "those who try to use marijuana as a medical treatment risk legal action by the U.S. Drug Enforcement Administration or other federal agencies and that the state laws provide no defense." (Lane, 2005)

Life Application Exercise #3

As I have pointed out, I myself am not perfect. But learning from my mistakes and having a plan for the future has helped me tremendously. Over time I have developed a personal ethical vision for myself based on the following principles:

A.) Doing what is right is what matters most to me; above everything, it guides my decision-making.

B.) I will do my job to the best of my ability—no matter what.

C.) I must be courageous enough to hold myself and others accountable.

D.) I must remain positive. It is an honor to serve. Being negative is not an option.

Take some time to think about you. What are some of some guiding principles that have stayed with you and direct your decision-making and conduct?

Chapter 5

Temptation and the Criminal Justice Field:

Is It Too Much for You... or Are You Too Much for It?

People struggle with all sorts of temptations. My biggest temptation is cheesecake. Set a piece before me, and there is a 99.9% likelihood that it will disappear. My most effective way to deal with this is avoidance. But this is tough at fancy sit-down dinners or high-end buffets, where the cheesecake inevitably beckons.

I assure you that I have other weaknesses, but I use cheesecake as an example because it presents a situation wherein willpower can fail. We must identify how damaging the consequences of giving in to temptation can be to our career choices. Just as my weakness for cheesecake should preclude my seeking employment at a bakery, so, too, should certain temptations give one pause before attempting to enter the criminal justice field.

Most modern-day corruption can be traced to one or both of two temptations—money and drugs. These can be exacerbated by other personal circumstances, such as work dissatisfaction, disillusionment, family problems, and financial trouble. Most of us encounter one or more of these circumstances at some point in our life, yet we manage to remain corruption-free. In my experience as a criminal justice professional, corruption risk can be categorized as one of three types.

1.) **The Surreptitious Offender**—having displayed a heretofore undiscovered but regular pattern of illegal behavior[6] prior to employment in the criminal justice field, this individual may seek to use his or her position to enhance opportunities for criminal activity.

2.) **The Borderline Temptee**—an individual not inclined to engage in criminal behavior, but who might be tempted to do so on a situational basis—depending on personal circumstances (e.g., financial hardship, dissatisfaction with work) and assessment of risk.

3.) **The Disciplined Do-Righter**—an individual who resists any kind of temptation that could lead to corruption. You could put this person in a room with a million dollars, and even if he or she has a child who needs an expensive operation to survive, it will remain untouched.

No one can really know the breakdown of this typology among criminal justice professionals, but the surreptitious offender and the borderline temptee probably represent a minority. The common motivator in many cases appears to be either money or drugs, or both, and in law enforcement, there are many opportunities to see large amounts of these kinds of plunder when an arrest is made or when a search warrant is executed. There are individuals who love drugs and money so much that they will do anything to obtain them. If this is you, steer clear of the criminal justice field.

Other temptations exist in just about every area of public service. There are those working in the criminal justice field who, for monetary gain, sometimes allow themselves to be bribed by outsiders with criminal intent. Examples include correctional officers, compliance personnel, and probation officers paid to look the other way as contraband is smuggled and violations are committed. Sadly, history is filled with police officers bribed by criminals to provide for the protection of illegal enterprises from the real "good guys." And it is not unusual for a drug trafficking organization to offer thousands of dollars to a border patrol agent to do nothing more than wave a vehicle through the border. No matter the amount, if you can be bought at any price, you should avoid working within the criminal justice system.

The temptations of money and drugs are closely linked. They share a profit connection: Drugs are a valuable commodity that can be liquidated. And both drugs and

---

[6] As a CRJ major, you may be familiar with the theories of deterrence. In the area of certainty of punishment, it is thought that as people engage in criminal behavior and do not face "certain punishment" because they are not detected or arrested, they come to believe that they can engage in criminal behavior without being caught.

greed can be intoxicating. Most law enforcement positions present many opportunities to interact with drug evidence, so it is not unreasonable to conclude that individuals who have used drugs illegally may have difficulty working in the criminal justice field.

Criminal justice agencies must ensure that new hires are not active addicts whose habit may interfere with work responsibilities, compromise investigations, and jeopardize the work and well-being of co-workers. But even recovering addicts who have been clean for a time may "fall off the wagon" if exposed to seized drugs—and agencies are understandably wary of those with a past history of abuse.

Life Application Exercise #1

Temptations are a part of life—and different stimuli pose struggles for many of us. Examine yourself and your lifestyle, and evaluate anything that you believe can present a potential weakness. Be honest with yourself and assess whether these weaknesses could affect your ability to maintain integrity in a criminal justice position.

Life Application Exercise #2

In the criminal justice field, especially law enforcement, large amounts of money and illegal drugs may be found at crime scenes and processed as evidence—potentially inviting corruption. Based on the typology of corruption discussed above, which of the three profiles most closely fits you? Before pursuing criminal justice as a career, you need to answer this for yourself. You do not have to tell anyone else.

You may shrug off your past instances of inappropriate or illegal behavior or actions as trivial, but do not minimize. Studies of corruption (including Barker, 1974) suggest that people who engage in less serious offenses often advance to more serious ones. And Gilmartin (1998) found that corrupt officers typically engage in acts of omission before turning to criminal commissions. Corruption can begin as small as a code of conduct infraction and escalate from there.

If you have given in to temptation and knowingly engaged in corrupt behavior, do yourself a favor: pursue a major other than CRJ! Because if you manage to enter the criminal justice field, you will risk bringing shame on yourself, your family, and your co-workers.

Chapter 6

Integrity

Integrity is your most valuable asset. By guarding your integrity, you also are maintaining your hireability. If you plan to pursue a career in criminal justice, take early steps to ensure that your behavior and actions are not questioned later. Avoid anything that would lead a prospective employer to conclude that your judgment is flawed.[7]

Perhaps the best way to measure integrity is to observe how one behaves when he or she thinks no one else is observing. When one knows he or she is being observed, behavior may be consciously modified for "show." If the boss is looking, people will usually be on their best behavior. Individuals with strong integrity do the right thing regardless of whether *anyone* is watching.

While an observer may be able to assess integrity through behavior, it is more difficult to judge what is going on in one's mind or heart. This is why self-screening is important: only you can be honest enough with yourself to determine whether you can be counted on to do the right thing—especially in a career that is likely to present many opportunities to do the wrong thing without observation or detection, and often therefore without consequence.

Here is something to consider: If your employer provided you a credit line for work-related expenses, could you be relied upon not to use the card for personal expenditures—even in the case of an emergency? Unfortunately, many agencies that have entrusted employees with official credit cards have dealt with unauthorized use or fraud in varying degrees. One scandal detailed in the 2002 General Accounting Office (GAO) report concerned significant cheating on travel and purchase cards issued by the Pentagon (*The New York Times*, 2002). The GAO's figures indicated that

---

[7] See Appendix A, "Choosy Bosses Choose the Ethically Marketable," for more on this topic.

over 45,000 Defense Department (DoD) employees, including some 700 military officers, had defaulted on at least $62 million in official credit card expenses charged to the government. Acknowledging "instances involving fraud, misuse and abuse of [credit cards], the Under Secretary of Defense created a Task Force to propose recommendations to strengthen the credit card program." (Zakheim, 2002)

While misusing a credit card given you by a friend or family member may strain the relationship, consequences in a criminal justice position may be more far-reaching. For government employees punishment for card misuse and fraud can include termination or demotion, imprisonment, probation, restitution, and revocation of security clearances. If you believe you would be tempted to use a corporate credit card personally, consider whether you want to subject yourself to a temptation that may result in firing, jail, or probation.

Operating in the Grey

While using official credit cards for personal use is conspicuously wrong, some people engage in bad behavior that is less obvious. Someone who frequently appears to be straddling the line between right and wrong—who exhibits behavior that is distasteful albeit legal I'll refer to as a "greyhound." Those planning to work or already working in this profession need to consider whether they prefer operating more in shades of grey than in black and white.

The criminal justice field will present many opportunities for engaging in behavior that will go unquestioned and situations where only you know the circumstances. For example, I had lunch with a couple who owned a business and were accustomed to stretching things a little on their taxes. During this entirely social outing, these greyhounds mentioned their business in passing—and then stated that since they broached it, this justified their classification of the lunch as a "business meal" for tax purposes. How would the Internal Revenue Service ever know the truth?

A useful self-assessment of personal ethics is to consider if you have taken postures similar to that of these tax-evading business owners. Have you violated a trust? If the answer is yes, then criminal justice may not be a good career choice for you.

Life Application Exercise #1

Based on your life experience to this point, you may not have been entrusted with a government-issued credit card and the responsibility to protect your employer's reputation—and your own—through its use. However, you likely have had opportunities to uphold or violate trusts placed in you by others. Think about the following questions and answer honestly. Your responses will help you determine whether your integrity is high or low and may identify weaknesses you can address prior to entering the criminal justice field.

Has a friend or family member entrusted you with their credit card and instructed you to use it for a particular purpose, and without permission you used it for another purpose? Have you ever over-extended parameters (e.g. cell phone minutes used, texting charges), substantially above the limit your parents or others set for you when they were paying your bills? Have you ever been instructed by your employer or parents to stop making telephone calls to certain numbers with expensive services (like 900 numbers)? Have you run up internet access or pay-per-view cable TV charges to the point your parents or other guardians had to enter into payment plans to continue service?

There are likely to have been times when family members, friends, or employers expressed disappointment in your decision-making. Did you learn from your mistakes, develop self-discipline, and try to do better? Or did your parents or employer have to institute certain blocking mechanisms to correct your behavior? If the answer to the last question is yes, you need to decide if you can handle working under rules and within ethical boundaries.

Life Application Exercise #2

Consider that administrators in different types of professions are likely to handle the same set of employee circumstances quite differently. There are, for example, wide variances between employers across industries when illegal drug use is detected in the workforce. Medical doctors caught using are encouraged to seek treatment whereas drug enforcement agents would be expected to resign or be fired. Most of us would agree that it is just as important for physicians to be as sober as police officers, but the factors of public service and agency subculture enter into how such problems are handled in the criminal justice field. Compare a criminal justice position you desire to a job outside of the field and how employee discipline may be handled after a violation of trust or criminal act. Did your analysis reveal that the criminal justice professional is usually held to a higher standard?

Chapter 7

Can You Keep a Secret?

When people confide their innermost thoughts to you, do you find it hard to keep them to yourself? In the criminal justice field, most employers require a significant degree of confidentiality from their practitioners. While some of your work may eventually become public knowledge, much information—such as trade secrets or classified intelligence about ongoing operations—is never made public.

Some employers will require written promises to keep sensitive information confidential as a condition of employment. Often this pledge will include a clause wherein you acknowledge that criminal or civil penalties are associated with any unauthorized disclosures. Unfortunately, not everyone making a pledge to remain quiet about sensitive information is sincere. And sadly, unauthorized disclosures can create negative consequences.

It is true that "loose lips can sink ships." In cases where an investigation does not conclude as planned or expected, chances are good that somewhere along the way confidentiality was compromised. This most commonly occurs when personnel lapse into indiscretion around individuals who have no need to know. A case ending in a failed prosecution due to unauthorized disclosures is bad enough, but more seriously troubling is when the unchecked chattiness of criminal justice practitioners jeopardizes the lives of undercover personnel.

Recognize the need for confidentiality in furtherance of your agency's mission, because discussing your work excessively can have a dire outcome. For example, reputed spy and former counter intelligence FBI agent Robert Hansen reported two double agents to his Russian handlers. Both were subsequently executed. (Havill, 2001)

Like Hansen, most law enforcement officers have access not only to sensitive information from the investigations they control but information that is contained in district- or agency-wide electronic indices. Criminal justice professionals populate and access various electronic databases filled with facts about criminals and their activities; and they are entrusted to query systems that contain millions of data about past as well as ongoing investigative activity in the course of their work. Often scattered throughout police and prosecution files is potentially embarrassing and private material about people who may have brief contact with police.

Persons not formally charged or who have had their records expunged are not considered criminals. However, investigative information could still be stored in archives that may be illegally queried by corrupt practitioners for private gain. Take, for instance, a California officer charged with tapping internal computer files to track female movie stars. The officer learned about any contacts his targets may have had with the police and then threatened them with public disclosure if they did not pay him. (Singer, 2003) Tabloid media hungry for exclusives on the famous have long fueled the market for internal police data.

Not every unauthorized search or disclosure is monetarily motivated. Improper queries can, for example, be used to check out a love interest. (If you feel compelled to investigate a person you are dating, chances are that you are probably already having second thoughts.) Do not risk your job by conducting unauthorized criminal history checks for yourself or anyone else. You will be expected not only to avoid intentional disclosures but to use caution to avoid unintentional ones—the kind that may fuel gossip within your family and/or social circle. Regardless of motivation or intent, criminal justice practitioners that make unauthorized queries and disclosures subject themselves to criminal and civil liability as well as internal sanctions. And above all, breaches of confidentiality are potentially dangerous.

Life Application Exercise #1

Are you guilty of TMI (too much information)? Do you convey information to others that you had previously decided not to reveal or that you are not required to reveal? Is this information more often about you or is it information that others have confided in you? Have you ever made a disclosure that you do not believe you should have that resulted in serious adverse consequences for others?

Life Application Exercise #2

Not all secrets are created equal. In May 2011, U.S. President Barack Obama announced that Osama bin Laden was detected and neutralized by U.S. Special Forces in Pakistan. Bin Laden is arguably the most infamous fugitive in history as a result of his being the self-proclaimed mastermind of the September 11, 2001 terrorist attacks on American soil. He had remained at large for almost ten years. It was disclosed that only a small number of people knew about this coup in its planning stages, which spanned several months. If you were one of the few in the know, could you have been counted on to keep this critical mission a secret?

Life Application Exercise #3

So entrusted are those holding security clearances that just one professional's failure to keep classified information secret can pose a threat to national security. In 2010, an army private was formally charged with leaking what was believed to be hundreds of thousands of classified documents to the anti-secrecy website WikiLeaks. The primary motivation of the accused was thought to be idealism: He wanted the government to be more transparent. Do you think employees should have the right to release secret information if they do not believe the information should be secret?

In response to this massive leak, government employees and CRJ majors have been warned not to review the classified information that can now be found in open sources. (O'Keefe, 2010) How do you feel about being told not to review the material? Can you curtail your curiosity given that no one is likely to know if you ever checked? Do you believe that being told to avoid this material is overkill, especially considering that non-government workers and those not majoring in CRJ are not held to the same standard?

Chapter 8

Associations: Family, Friends and Others Close

Do not be misled, bad company corrupts good character.
—NIV Bible, 1 Corinthians 15:33

Associations—they can make or break you. What others do in your presence, particularly when there are negative consequences, can affect your ability to obtain employment in the criminal justice field. This chapter will help you identify the type of aberrant behavior to avoid in others and provide the rationale behind the profession's requirement that employees eliminate personal contact with criminals.

Basically, you need be careful when it comes to admitting people into your social sphere. Let's say you are out with friends, they are committing crimes, and you do nothing about it. You may face repercussions. Juveniles or people working outside of criminal justice may merely be inconvenienced by bad behavior, but professionals such as sworn law enforcement officers may be required to take action if criminal acts occur in their presence—pursuant to their organization's on-duty/off-duty guidelines. Negative publicity for the agency can also result if individuals who are seen as criminals are mixing with those charged with upholding the law.

Another concern for law enforcers and their agencies: associating with criminals at any time can jeopardize investigations and prosecutions. Individuals associating with criminals are also susceptible to blackmailers seeking official favors.

Before entering into an association with someone, take into consideration whether this person frequently gets into trouble, especially with the law. Fighting, cheating, and stealing are regarded as bad behavior for a juvenile; for adults, they become the criminal acts of assault, fraud, larceny, and robbery. (Keep in mind that once a person reaches the age of 18, he or she is regarded as an adult.[8]) It follows that an offense such as criminal gang activity will carry great legal consequence for those charged as adults.

A risk of interacting with known or borderline criminals is that you may be drawn into illegal activities of which you are unaware. Drug trafficking is a good example. Entrepreneurs of the drug world often create a legitimate business front to conceal their underground dealings, and if you are unaware of this, you may unwittingly become involved. What if you go out with a friend who tells you he is stopping to visit associates when in reality he is dropping off drugs or picking up dirty money? Absent this knowledge, you could unwittingly become entangled.

If detained, you may think, *The police will figure out that I was not really involved in anything illegal—what's the harm?* Fortunately for those duped, police are usually savvy enough to distinguish between the directly culpable and those on the periphery in a given situation. However, if you are the one "left holding the bag," your chances for "taking the rap"—i.e., prosecution—increase. Avoid being naive and realize that even if you are detained briefly and then released, there usually is some record kept of your detention.

The effect a detention in your background may have on your employment prospects varies within the criminal justice field. Frequently, detentions are only contained in the internal files of the agency making the contact. But if you seek employment with an agency that has intelligence on you, doubt is cast. The sensitivity of the position will determine the depth of the investigation and sources used. Also consider that if the hiring agency has no knowledge or access to the internal databases of another agency, certain background questionnaires may require you to disclose detentions even if there is no record of it.

Of course, anyone would consider it unfair to have employment opportunities blocked just for being in the wrong place at the wrong time. But the fact is that a lot of people are vying for a limited number of criminal justice jobs. This means at each stage of the process, hiring managers are looking for additional screens to help reduce the candidate pool to a manageable number. The best way to avoid being kicked to the curb is by preparing early and being wary of questionable behavior.

Dealings that may be harder to gauge concern goods sold in nontraditional outlets. You do not even have to be in the proverbial "wrong place" to be faced with having the opportunity to purchase "hot stuff"—and being susceptible to arrest for receiving stolen goods. I have even been solicited in beauty shops by people peddling an assortment of merchandise. But even their possession of a vendor's license does

---

[8] Depending on the severity of a crime, some jurisdictions may opt to charge minors as adults.

not guarantee that they are legitimate salespeople. Use caution when making purchases from street vendors, flea markets, garage sales, and yes, eBay.

So you don't think you have friends as described above? Perhaps you don't—but you do not want to find out the hard way that you are wrong. Your future career is worth it for you to try and learn as much as you can about the character of your friends and not ignore warning signs.

This subject is trickier to address when applied to family. You can choose friends, but you cannot choose family members. Family is an institution into which you are born. From parents to siblings to cousins, when family is involved in criminal behavior it becomes personal. You may have encountered situations wherein a family member's behavior has made you uncomfortable. Although you may not be personally involved in their activities, you have wondered if maybe a time would come when the police will swoop down on them and you possibly could get caught in the middle. Perhaps certain family members are involved in something potentially violent, such as gang activity or drug dealing, and you have felt endangered. What do you do when you have a family member who is breaking the law?

I once listened to a radio talk show devoted to a discussion of family and crime. The consensus was that if a family member criminally offends, creating problems for you personally, the best thing to is to avoid or at least minimize contact with that individual so that you are not in harm's way. This is sound advice even if you are not seeking employment in the criminal justice field. Any at rate, merely being related to an offender should not pose serious career problems; just be prepared to discuss the amount of time you have spent with a convicted family member as part of the hiring process.

That said, it bears repeating: your continuing association with someone engaged in criminal behavior, even if it is a family member, can adversely impact your career and tarnish the agency's reputation. An example of this kind of scenario involved a military officer who was assigned to a South American country in charge of the U.S. counter-narcotics effort there. During this duty, his wife was arrested for sending heroin back to the United States. (Feuer, 2000) How do you think this scandal affected her husband's career, the military branch of government that he served, and the U.S. and South American perception of this counter-narcotics effort?

In fact, this incident brought embarrassment and shame to the husband and his employer as there was substantial press coverage. Making the story more newsworthy was the high-level position of the drug importer's husband: each time there was a court action, the story made headlines anew. The lesson? While you personally may not be involved with a family member's bad behavior, you can feel the ill effects of his or her trespasses—especially if you share a roof with that person. Some employers

—aware of the temptation a criminal justice employee may have to use his or her position to aid a family member—withhold or withdraw a security clearance if it is determined that you have someone living with you engaged in illegal behavior.

Here is another real-life scenario, using fictitious names: When Brandy was hired as a police officer, the fact that her father was a reputed drug dealer was not held against her. Brandy married Tony, a sergeant assigned to narcotics. Eventually, Tony compromised an investigation in order to protect the criminal activities of his wife's dad. Brandy and Tony were terminated. If you are unable to separate personal attachment from professional responsibility, avoid criminal justice work.

Romantic relationships are even more vulnerable. Significant others combine the traits of associates and family: you chose them and then they became family, or certainly like family. Spouses and cohabitants are of interest to prospective criminal justice employers because of the influence they can have on a candidate. To be certain, live-in love interests will be intensely scrutinized if you are subject to a background investigation.

Your choice of a mate is a point around which others will form opinions about you. Examining your partner's character can reveal how responsible you are, what you are willing to tolerate, and what you forbid. Illegal behavior displayed by one's mate will reveal your willingness to condone it. A criminal justice employer may therefore conclude that the recruit is irresponsible—posing more of a risk than is acceptable for the position.

Because your associations can impact your criminal justice career, there are restrictions. As soon as you decide that you will pursue a position in this field, take stock of your connections and sever yourself from those who are actively involved in criminal offending—knowing that the best policy is to avoid such associations to begin with. And remember that criminal links not identified during the hiring process can surface later and result in dismissal.

All of this may seem very restrictive and too much of a sacrifice. If you feel this way, recognize it early so that you do not waste time pursuing a degree in a field in which you will not be comfortable working. If much of what you have read thus far is not a problem for you—then go for it!

Life Application Exercise #1

To help you explore the dynamics of how you and your employer might regard personal associations, imagine this: You are visiting extended family, and suddenly there is a raid at the house. The police come in with weapons and point them at you and instruct you to stay on the floor. They identify you and then order you to sit on the sofa, where you remain until they complete a search of the house and discover contraband. Would you feel that it was worth it to spend time with people who have put you in this kind of jeopardy? How do you think your supervisor will react when you call and make such a notification to them? Bear in mind that your name and professional position may wind up in the newspaper.

Think about it. This situation may seem difficult or unfair, but are you willing and able to deal with its reality? Are you a realist or an idealist? You certainly can be both on a situational basis, but your involvement in a situation such as this would test your ability to deal with both perception and reality.

Life Application Exercise #2

Much of our discussion about associations and friends involves common sense. When I was a teen, I realized that I had a cousin who had sticky fingers. The first time a security guard grabbed her as we left a store, I was very defensive and called her mother immediately to complain that she was being treated unfairly. However, after the second time, I concluded that my cousin was a thief, and realizing the possible trouble into which she could land me, I never went shopping with her again.

Think about relatives you believe are involved in criminal offending. Could their activities adversely affect your credibility or ability to work in the criminal justice field? How? Do you believe you should limit your contact with these particular relatives? The good news is that you will not automatically be disqualified from a position merely because you have family members who have engaged in criminality or are currently incarcerated. But questions may be raised nonetheless. The answers you give may factor into your perceived suitability to hold a criminal justice position—where the primary focus will remain on your own behavior.

Chapter 9
Loyalty

Are you more loyal to your friends or to your employer? Where do you stand when these loyalties conflict? Perhaps in other jobs, leaning one way or the other was never an issue. But if your employer is a criminal justice agency, at times you may have to decide whether to keep promises you made to your employer or maintain a friendship or other close relationship.

So mission-critical is the loyalty of criminal justice practitioners that often an oath is administered upon commencement of a new position. Basically, the pledge is an acknowledgement that you will uphold the guiding charter of the branch of government in which you will work (e.g., the U.S. Constitution, if you become a federal worker). Your employer will expect and demand your loyalty as you discharge your duties.

As a criminal justice professional, you may observe the public regularly both out in front and behind the scenes—increasing the possibility that your career may intersect with the life of someone you know personally. That's when the loyalty test is presented.[9] From detecting private financial information about neighbors to witnessing misconduct on the part of your dentist, details can be revealed unexpectedly. The key to navigating these situations is a pre-established personal commitment to keep quiet. You should already have settled in your mind and heart that should you ever encounter information about a person you know, your next step is to exhibit loyalty to your oath. I have found the best practice is to inform the appropriate officials of the agency so that you may be extricated from the case to eliminate conflict of interest.

---

[9] For more about ethical tests, see Appendix B, "The Most Important Test is Pass/Fail."

Keeping silent about your connection to investigative targets will not eliminate trouble; in fact, informing your boss about a potential conflict of interest allows your agency to plan how to minimize your involvement in a scenario that may have adverse consequences for both you and the agency. For example, your presence at an arrest scene may be so inflammatory that friends you consider loyal may attempt to save their own hides by alleging your involvement in their criminal activities. Make no mistake: You, as a criminal justice professional, will always be viewed as a "bigger fish" than an ordinary criminal. (I personally believe that it should be a criminal justice manager's priority to root out criminals posing covertly as police, prosecutors, etc., within their ranks.)

Sometimes criminal justice professionals experience divided loyalties when they believe employers engage in unfair practices. Racial profiling and mistakes such as detaining the wrong suspect or raiding the wrong house have motivated criminal justice professionals to side against their agencies. And at some point you, too, may feel that a friend or relative is incapable of what they have been accused of and is being "railroaded" by your agency. Rather than trying to single-handedly level the playing field, immediately disclose your associations and/or concerns to your supervisor.

Life Application Exercise #1

You have just learned that your agency plans to arrest a relative or one of your closest friends in two days by raiding his home and seizing all valuable property suspected of being purchased with ill-gotten gains. What would you do?

Alerting an individual to an impending law enforcement action is not only poor conduct for a criminal justice professional, it is illegal. One could be charged with obstruction of justice for such at tip-off. Moreover, you could even face more extreme adverse consequences, such as being expected to make financial restitution for the value of the lost assets that were targeted for seizure.

Life Application Exercise #2

As a criminal justice professional, how would you respond if a close friend or relative told you that he used your name and profession as a bluff to get someone to confess to a previous arrest. Specifically, you are informed that the third party was told you checked them out.

Life Application Exercise #3

A news story about two brothers—one a prominent university president, the other a notorious criminal (Friedman, 2003)—presents an example of an ethical dilemma involving family and crime. Because the criminal brother was reported as a fugitive, the university president came under scrutiny as to his role in facilitating his brother's evasion of the police. It is believed by some that the university president had contact with his brother that he refused to disclose. For this reason, some demanded the university president's removal.[10]

If the suspicions about him were true, perhaps the university president wanted to help his brother. But try viewing this situation from different moral and relationship angles. What would you do in this situation? An important question for the CRJ major is whether you would be willing to do right by the job even if your action would be viewed negatively by family.

Probably the best example of this involved David Kaczynski's turning in of his brother, Theodore Kaczynski—the infamous "Unabomber" who was convicted of killing and injuring numerous people in multiple attacks through mailed explosives. David, a social worker who recognized similarities between Ted's ideas and a manifesto distributed to and published by newspapers, has spoken publicly about turning in his brother to save lives. His loyalty to society trumped his loyalty to his brother; he even went so far as to contact Ted's victims to express his family's grief over the suffering they had endured. (Harris, 1999)

Keep in mind that a law enforcement officer is obligated to report criminal activity that others may not. An officer could be brought up on charges and subsequently dismissed for failure to fulfill this basic duty.

---

[10] The university president later resigned under political pressure. (Kellogg, 2003)

Chapter 10
Truth and Honesty

Did you know that as a criminal justice professional your "word" will be so revered—whether delivered verbally or in writing—that it will be required for any number of legal applications? It may be used in affidavits to influence a judge to order a search and seizure warrant to raid someone's home. It may be needed to carry out an arrest. In some states, it may be needed as part of the death penalty order of a convicted murderer. All of these applications require uncompromised truth. Even a little inaccuracy or exaggeration is unacceptable when someone's life hangs in the balance.

The criminal justice system employs professionals to gather and analyze facts and then reach conclusions. While those practitioners are not the ultimate determiner of truth (i.e., judge or jury), their assessments can result in adverse actions for others as it relates to degree of charges, arrest, conviction, etc. Since these are such serious matters, those seeking to work in the criminal justice field should not only determine if they want a job with important duties, but also gauge their own ability to be scrupulous in their evaluations of people and circumstances.

When there is no corroboration available, the truth of a matter may be determined solely on the criminal justice practitioner's perspective or recollection of events. Criminal justice professionals therefore must reject any temptation to misrepresent facts, even if those facts will make them or their agencies look bad. This begs the question: If you tell a lie and no one knows or can prove it is a lie—is it still a lie? The answer is *yes*. And the more a person lies, the easier it becomes to repeat the behavior in the future—making habitual lying a slippery slope. [11]

---

[11] This suggests that corruption is the result of a continuum where less serious compromises occur before more serious offenses.

Unfortunately, evidence suggests untruthfulness is common. An interview with Gregg Behr, founding director of the North Carolina based Content of Our Character Project, revealed that 93 percent of high school students surveyed reported lying at least once to their teachers and their parents. (Ellin, 2003) Moreover, 37 percent said they would lie to get a job.

While avoiding unpleasant outcomes is a common motive for untruthfulness, telling the truth is the best practice—and it may not always result in the expected negative consequence. And besides, there always exists the possibility that lies will be uncovered. This can be stressful for the person who told the lie—leading to distraction from personal life and work. This can be particularly difficult when one presents falsehoods as a basis for entry into the criminal justice field.

With no statute of limitations on lying, gains are illusory because you can lose them. In other words, if lying permitted you to get the job, if it is later detected, it can cost you the position. Consider Mary Brown's (not her true name) quest to be hired by the U.S. Treasury Department as a Customs Inspector. Initially she was selected for a position, but after revealing that she used marijuana and cocaine and sold marijuana as a teen, the offer was rescinded. Brown's subsequent legal battle argued that her juvenile misdeeds should not have disqualified her. After several rulings, Brown ultimately was denied the position. The prevailing decision was based upon an updated (and undoubtedly more thorough) background investigation that revealed thefts occurring when she was an adult; and her falsely answering no to a question about relatives' involvement in crime.[12]

Just as omitting or concealing negative information from your past may create problems for your future, exaggerations can also prove damaging. I am aware of one law enforcement professional who ruined his career by misrepresenting past employment as a state police trooper in sworn documents. And when I joined Detroit's police force as a local officer in 1978, the city—then proactively hiring individuals receiving public assistance—had a problem with new employees continuing to collect welfare when they were no longer eligible. These were otherwise "nice people" whose dishonesty cost them their jobs and gave the police department a tarnished reputation.

Fraud is a particularly alluring crime to which even the criminally disinclined are susceptible. Virtually everyone is enticed at some point to engage in illegal deceit because it is typically viewed as a convenient solution. Consider some general examples of how easy it is to engage in fraud despite potentially escalating consequences:

---

[12] MSPB, SF073101044711, 9/30/03. (*Federal Employees News Digest*, November 24, 2003).

• Reporting the "lemon" automobile you bought as stolen or accidentally destroyed in order for the insurance company to pay it off and apply funds to the purchase of a new vehicle.

• Stating that you live with a rich uncle in order to lower your insurance premiums or gain access for your children to a better school.

• Pretending to be more incapacitated than you really are as a result of a work-related accident in order to receive time off and disability compensation.

• Fudging, even just a little, on your tax return.

Procedures and case law have evolved to handle illegal instances of lying. To whom one lies, and under what circumstances, can be weighed in determining whether a person is allowed to retain a job or be criminally prosecuted.[13] Criminal court cases have also brought clarity to defendants' rights. Two of them are the Giglio and Henthorn decisions.[14] In Giglio, it was determined that the defense is entitled to know about credibility concerns that have arisen on the part of prosecution witnesses. And in Henthorn the mechanism for satisfying the Giglio requirement was established by perusing the personnel files of criminal justice personnel slated to testify. (Schott, 2003)

Since the Henthorn ruling, agencies have tended to disqualify candidates suspected to have been untruthful and dismiss or reassign practitioners caught in lies or lacking candor. Where previously some employers may have been inclined to excuse behavior, it is now more apparent that employees with a credibility problem can adversely impact an agency's ability to carry out its functions and missions.

Criminal justice agencies' dependency on honesty means that hopefuls must embrace this quality. You should always strive to be completely truthful. Remember: the veracity of your words is always subject to testing.

---

[13] At the center of the charges filed against celebrity homemaker Martha Stewart in 2003 is that she lied to authorities. Her trial and conviction included a breach of criminal justice ethics as well: a government witness at the trial was charged with perjury in his testimony about the examination of forensic evidence. (Farrell, 2004)

[14] *Giglio v. United States,* 405 U.S.150(1972); and *Henthorn v. United States,* 931 F.2d 29 (9th Circuit 1991).

Life Application #1

Think about a few times when you have not been truthful. Think about the outcomes. That you can remember these instances suggests that you felt some guilt then, and perhaps still do, even if no one detected your dishonesty. Try to forgive yourself and move on; if you cannot, it may be time to seek professional help or consider exposing the facts to the appropriate people. Remember the lingering bad aftertaste of lying so that you can endeavor to avoid it in the future.

Life Application Exercise #2

Pete Rose is probably now as well-known for illegally betting on professional baseball as he is for being one of the game's top players. Rose had always denied engaging is such unethical activity until early 2004, when he publicly admitted his wrongdoing—tarnishing his own reputation as well as that of the sport. Do you believe his final revelation should or has changed anything? Your observation should include what you believe the proper authorities should have done.

Chapter 11

The Gateway: Electronic Communications and You

The digital frontier—namely online social networking and electronic communications—is fraught with peril for criminal justice professionals and those seeking employment in the field. Because a Google search has virtually become a routine application processing step for employers, ensuring a reputable result in the electronic realm is as important as keeping a clean record elsewhere.

A frequent misperception held by those who have immersed themselves in electronic communications—and by now, by either choice or necessity, this is virtually all of us—is that messages and information exchanged privately will forever be confidential or somehow "evaporate" over time. The truth is that if you electronically transmit messages, photographs, or other material, there is a possibility that at some point a prospective employer, an investigator or someone else will locate or gain access to them. You are, in effect, leaving a digital footprint.

As we delve into this discussion, know that how you exercise the protections afforded you under the U. S. Constitution can be a double-edged sword. The First Amendment provides for freedom of speech: with few exceptions, such as inciting a panic, you can say whatever you want verbally or in writing whenever you wish. However, this protection does not extend to the *consequences* of free speech: as any politician knows, what you say publicly can have repercussions on your career.

Text Messaging

Most of us are comfortable that our telephone conversations are private primarily because there is usually no permanent record (such as through taping) of what was precisely said. Yet a written record, whether in hard copy or digital form, should never be afforded the same level of privacy expectation.

An example: Graphic text messages between former Detroit Mayor Kwame Kilpatrick and his chief of staff, Christine Beatty—both married—landed them in hot water professionally. While their affair in and of itself was not a criminal offense, Kilpatrick and Beatty gave false statements under oath about the nature of their relationship. When evidence of the text messages surfaced several years later, they were not only prosecuted, but two promising legal careers were damaged—probably irreparably. Both were convicted and sentenced to jail time. Additionally, pursuant to his pleadings, Kilpatrick forfeited his law license.

The increasing frequency of text message-based scandals illustrates the importance of being mindful of the content of your electronic exchanges. Normally the Fourth Amendment, which protects people from unreasonable searches and seizure, would keep the government and others from being able to snoop through your digital correspondence—but if a warrant is obtained, all bets are off. Moreover, your own actions—like forwarding messages to third parties—can negate your legal protections, as they may be interpreted that you had already given up any reasonable expectation of privacy.

Consider a relevant 2010 case in which the U.S. Supreme Court decisively backed public sector employers. The Ontario Police Department (California) determined that Officer Jeff Quon had text communications between he, his ex-wife, and his girlfriend stored on a work-furnished device. Subsequently disciplined for this conduct, Quon sued—alleging that his privacy had been violated—and the case went all the way to the Supreme Court. In its ruling, the high court found that "because the search of Quon's text messages was reasonable, petitioners did not violate respondents' Fourth Amendment rights."[15] The Supreme Court's finding was made despite the fact that the employer permitted limited personal communications; it was the *content* of the messages that violated police department protocol.

Email

Email has become a common and convenient form of communication. But be mindful that it may become a permanent record able to be viewed by others besides the intended recipient. All it takes is a click of a mouse to forward your message to a large number of people; with serial forwarding, a private message can quickly become very, very public. This reason, and the almost weekly stories in the media about celebrities and politicians having their private lives and bad behavior exposed via email they thought was private, should convince you to temper the content and tone

---

[15] *City of Ontario, California, et al. v. Quon*, No. 08-1332 (2010).

of your electronic communications. In 2011, Congressmen Anthony Weiner and Christopher Lee resigned in disgrace after their online communications revealed intimate messages and lewd photographs.

The use of a work email account for personal matters is especially risky. It is likely that work email accounts will be tracked, monitored, and/or reviewed by a system administrator. Another reason for not using your work email account for personal messages is the danger forwarded emails can pose politically. Sensitive positions such as those in the federal government prohibit use of government property or time for political actions, as described under the Hatch Act[16]—which has been used as a basis to discipline, terminate, or prosecute workers during election cycles.

Technological advances have made email tracking and source identification possible both in the workplace and on the Web. In the workplace, the proprietor of the server often claims ownership to all email contained therein. Some agencies issue written reminders that electronic messages do not belong to employees. Typically, sensitive work positions come with guidelines for use of work email accounts and require a written acknowledgement of the policies' understanding. So think twice before you send or forward any email.

Facebook, My Space, Personal Web Pages

Titillating personal ads and posts can be viewed on Web bulletin boards and personal pages every day. No big deal, right? Perhaps not to those who haven't faced consequences of such experiences.

It may also be fairly challenging for those who are casual in their cyberspace comportment to gauge the limits of modesty that employers may use to judge employee candidates. For this reason, you should research company websites and, if you can, locate the personal Web pages of their high-level managers to identify possible boundaries before you construct your Facebook, MySpace, and other personal online pages. Consider a tone that feels professionally appropriate, as opposed to fun and free-wheeling, as you fill in the various personality and relationship status blanks or share your interests, experiences, and photos on these sites. While it may be understood that many people, including those who are being considered for sensitive positions, are engaged in personal intimate relationships, it is unlikely the subject will come up in an interview or background investigation unless you bring it up in some way.

You may think there would be no reason to plan for a discussion of your sexual

---

[16] The Hatch Act (5 U.S.C. §§ 7321-7326) governs the political activity of federal civilian executive branch employees. While it generally permits most federal employees to actively participate in partisan political management and partisan political campaigns, covered employees, however, are prohibited from—among other things—engaging in political activity while on duty, in a government office or building, while wearing an official uniform, or using a government vehicle.

interests or exploits with a prospective employer; however, if you are broadcasting such information on the Web, it may become part of your pre-employment screening. Your personal Web pages need not be boring, but they do need to be modest if you are seeking work in sensitive positions overseen by managers with potentially conservative viewpoints. For example, as one previously involved in hiring decisions for federal positions, I found it disturbing to discover a gentleman in a sensitive work position bragging graphically on his Facebook page about the expected results of using a product designed to enhance sexual pleasure.

It is not just your own Web pages about which to be concerned. Entries you make in cyberspace about others, on the pages of others, and in public comment forums also can come back to haunt you. The same guidelines you impose upon yourself relative to the spoken word and social comportment should be employed when you commit comments to cyberspace—even if you think your remarks are being made anonymously. There always remains the possibility that anything that you write "incognito" about someone else in the comments section of a newspaper may be later disclosed as originating from you. In particular, you should think first about any negative comments made to a blog about a former employer. Some may argue that since true statements are not slander, you cannot realize any ill effects of a smear campaign; however, future employers may not be sympathetic to candidates behaving in this manner.

Twitter

If you follow the National Football League's (NFL) model relative to the use of Twitter, then you will be concerned about how and when to utilize the medium. The NFL set forth a policy establishing blackout periods that prohibit the use of Twitter and other social networks on game day by coaches, players, and operations personnel. (Maske, 2009) Ethical concerns about cyber-transmissions ranged from cheating if a planned play were prematurely conveyed to argumentative complaints about referees' calls.

The root issue is that Twitter can adversely impact your personal enterprise. First, consider that there are times when it is inappropriate for you to Tweet (or, for that matter, text-message or talk on the phone)—such as while driving or performing work that requires your undivided attention. If an accident occurs as a result of this distraction, electronic tracing will inevitably lead to you. For example, an air traffic controller was suspended after it was determined that he was engaged in a personal telephone call when a fatal mid-air collision between a helicopter and small airplane above the Hudson River occurred during his watch. (Bazinet, 2009) There have been numerous other incidents in mass transit involving injury or death when operators were distracted by engaging in unnecessary electronic communications.

Second, before engaging in Twitter or other real-time social-technical communications, be advised that you may be giving up protections afforded under the U.S. Constitution. The Privacy Act holds that other than in very restricted circumstances the government cannot disclose information it obtains about citizens. There's also the Right to Financial Privacy Act, which precludes financial institutions from disclosing your personal information except in narrowly defined circumstances. Your disclosures through Twitter—which can be read instantly by millions—remove an expectation of privacy and hence, your shelter under the law is no longer guaranteed.

Third, be aware that with any form of electronic communication glitches can occur and systems can be hacked—possibly exposing embarrassing or ruinous information to the public. Congressman Anthony Weiner initially blamed hacking for his inadvertent transmission of lewd and explicit photographs intended for one email recipient—a misrepresentation that was arguably the beginning of his downfall. Consider the degree of reliance you place on this form of transmission and the potential for inadvertently compromising or forfeiting your personal security. Once the horse is out of the barn, it's hard to get it back in.

Photographs

WARNING! Photographs of you nude, partially nude, consuming alcohol or drugs, or engaging in any lewd or deviant act may result in your exclusion from certain professional positions or dismissal from employment. Moreover, photographs of other persons in the aforementioned compromising positions that you electronically access or save on your employer's property may result in termination. Electronically possessing illegal material such as child pornography may result not only in termination but in prosecution under the law.

Thwarting detection has become something of an obsession among those who cannot resist online pornography. But attempts to erase Web search histories and hard drives can lead a digital forensic expert right to the offending or incriminating material. Technology has advanced so far that embedded data in electronic photographs can include the precise location of where the picture was taken. Additionally, when images show up on the internet, they seem to remain available to search engines indefinitely. Consistent with the advice offered throughout this book, resist such temptations and you will not have to worry.

A final word on electronic communications: this is one area of your life that is completely within your control. By virtue of what you publish via websites, text messaging, and email, you decide what you wish to reveal about yourself. Once data or information about you is voluntarily released to the public, there is little you can do to erase. Although we live in a nation with freedom of speech, you must take care to ensure that exercising this freedom does not restrict your career aspirations.

Be ever mindful that as you pursue work in the criminal justice field, you are vying for some of the most difficult-to-obtain positions available anywhere. You are not owed a job, and no one *has* to accommodate you. As frustrating as navigating the process may be, avoid declaring a "poison pen war" with recruiters, executives, secretaries, or any other person you interact with in any way relative to the process. The road to obtaining a criminal justice position is necessarily arduous but, if you are a successful candidate, can be as equally rewarding.

Life Application Exercise #1

Many of the ethical pitfalls referenced in this book involve sexual behavior. In my career-coaching experience, I have met individuals who are seeking or already working in sensitive job positions who are consumed by worry over the implications of intimate matters. Take a moment and consider your past and current sexual behavior—and ask yourself if anything you have done or are doing could possibly create difficulty in your ability to be hired or retain a sensitive criminal justice position. This includes "evidence" floating around in cyberspace about your private life that you posted voluntarily. Determine if you need to adjust either your behavior or your choice of career.

Life Application Exercise #2

No doubt you have heard about a notorious Facebook online survey asking whether respondents thought the President of the United States should be assassinated. While an ensuing Secret Service investigation concluded that the poll posed no threat, here is a pertinent question: Do you think that a law enforcement agency, after using all electronic investigation means at its disposal, would be likely to hire the person who had posted the poll or one who had responded affirmatively?

Life Application Exercise #3

Prepare a diary entry for a blog or Facebook page along with a personal photograph. Before posting the material, ask someone you regard as reserved to review it. The feedback you receive may discourage you from creating a colorful online presentation or keep you from using it to get a date, but it just may help you get or keep a good job.

Life Application Exercise #4

An urgent text message invites you to participate in a "flash rob." A mob is planning to storm a local electronics store in precisely thirty minutes, steal as much as possible, and then flee. Like other flash plots, conspirators are banking on their numbers to diminish getting caught. What would you do? What would you not do?

Part III

The Selection Process

Chapter 12
What to Expect

You can write the greatest job application. You can have the most impressive resume. You can ace the job interview like no other candidate because you are a gifted orator. But all of this will be in vain if you cannot pass the final test: a background check. Your failure to clear this last hurdle very likely means that you will *not* get the job.

A background check in most cases involves several screenings. These may include a urinalysis, fingerprinting, and a polygraph examination. Collectively, these screenings will bolster your prospective employer's belief that you are being truthful. As intrusive as these screenings can be, I believe in the future we can expect more. For example, a sure way to ensure that an applicant is not a suspect in a crime would be to conduct DNA testing in connection with a criminal-history check.

With the rigors of a background check in mind, it is as good a time as any to ponder your pursuit of a criminal justice career. You may be asking yourself: *Why is it so important that they look at me like I am under a microscope?* But you must accept that this is only the beginning of the constant scrutiny you will receive as a criminal justice professional. Some of the screenings you must endure prior to hire will continue to occur randomly and/or cyclically. Additional psychological or polygraph testing occurs if concerns about you develop or if you elect more sensitive assignments. If you are a very private person who will be uncomfortable with any of this, criminal justice may not be the best line of work for you.

Think for a moment about the power that you will exercise through your position in law enforcement, corrections, probation, or prosecution. Each of these authoritative entities requires their practitioners to make decisions about whether people will be exonerated or imprisoned (and for how long). Police officers are empowered to take a life in the line of duty if deemed absolutely necessary. With this kind of authority, responsibility, and discretion at your hand, it is essential that you are able to exercise sound judgment. It follows that you must be trustworthy and dependable in making critical, sometimes life-or-death decisions—hence, the rationale for thorough up-front and ongoing vetting.

While your entire behavioral history is relevant to this process, your conduct dur-ing the years you pursue a CRJ degree or an employment certification (such as from a police academy) is especially pertinent. A person on a criminal justice career track who repeatedly makes poor decisions with ethical or legal repercussions is evaluated more harshly. For example, experimentation with drugs or obtaining phony identi-fication to purchase alcohol are unwise things to do at any time; however, if done within view of pursuing a career in law enforcement, they are particularly egre-gious—and will surely call judgment into question. A criminal justice employer could reasonably conclude that a person making such poor choices, whether consciously or out of ignorance, is inherently unsuited to work in the field.

Surviving the multi-stage hiring process will test the candidate's stamina and pa-tience. In developing your endurance, it helps to know what to expect and some of the reasons why your prospective employers will appear so inquisitive. Agencies, as they should, invest a lot of time, energy, and money in making the right hires. Their failure to do so can be catastrophic. All it takes is one individual to tarnish the repu-tation and effectiveness of a criminal justice agency.

Chapter 13
Drugs—to Use or Not to Use?

Ethical fitness for a criminal justice career hinges on many factors that are within an aspirant's control. Central among them is illegal drug use. This is one of the most significant social issues in America today—with a substantial number of citizens having experimented with or becoming addicted to drugs. Virtually everyone will be provided with an opportunity to say yes or no to drugs at some point in their lives.

Past experimentation with drugs can potentially affect your goal to work in the criminal justice system—with evidence of addiction probably eliminating your chances to work as a law enforcement officer. Addicts are typically disqualified from policing because law enforcement officers are regularly exposed to narcotics during the course of their duties: it could be unwise for a former addict to be assigned to, or accept, a routine case involving drug evidence due to potential relapse. While you may know former addicts who have recovered, many criminal justice agencies view evidence of past drug use as a potential future susceptibility to corruption.

My best advice: If you have never experimented with drugs, then do not choose to do so. Making my own mind up at an early age, I have never tried drugs. And on those few occasions when I was a teen and marijuana was discussed, I made my stance clear to others and left if the drug was produced. Before long, everyone seemed to respect my decision even if it was not a socially popular one.

Due to the widespread availability of illegal substances, I recognize that avoiding them can be challenging. You must remain disciplined and vigilant—even if it means declining invitations to parties or other social situations where drug use is known or is likely to occur. Just being exposed to marijuana smoke can lead to second-hand inhalation and possibly a positive test result. A positive reading during any type of job application drug screening will likely be a disqualifying factor and jeopardize the positions of those already employed. Or, it may result in flat-out blacklisting from employment in the criminal justice field.

Realistically, a long-ago arrest for smoking a "joint" will not automatically eliminate all of your possible prospects in the field. Of more concern would be the potentially problematic personal interactions that led to the act. Criminal justice administrators justifiably are wary of job candidates or employees who associate in any way with those who sell or supply drugs. An admission of drug use therefore begs the question of the substance's origin.[1] Some employers may simply opt to play it safe and move on to the next candidate.

Life Application Exercise

Ask yourself these questions concerning drug use: Can it lead to addiction? Can it lead to arrest? Can it lead to associations which may interfere with my ability to obtain a criminal justice position?

---

[1] Past drug abusers seeking employment with the DEA will be asked to identify their suppliers.

Chapter 14

The Background Investigation: Getting to Know Who You Are

The primary purpose of a background investigation is for your prospective employer to get to know who you are—to establish some degree of confidence that you can be trusted. The good news: If you make it to this stage in the application process, it is a positive indicator that you are being seriously considered for the job, as a background investigation represents a costly investment in the candidate. It is the last assurance an employer seeks.

A background investigator will consider multiple sources in assembling your composite—much like a puzzle. Your history is checked from many different, privacy-invading angles, including some that will require your consent. Agencies that require background checks most likely will request that you sign release documents that will permit them to delve into various aspects of your past. Your refusal to sign any such waiver will likely be a red flag that you have something to hide. You can elect not to waive your rights, of course, but at the price of not being considered for the job.

The intrusion into an applicant's privacy rarely ends with hire, as some positions require periodic updated background checking indefinitely. There are even times when an investigation is launched outside of the regular cycle if there is an ethical violation or complaint.

There are several key areas where a background investigator will look.

Driving record

Drinking and driving is viewed negatively by our society, including many employers. Many criminal justice positions require you to drive a work vehicle. To that end, your driving history/record may play a part in the hiring decision. Due to risk, if you have a history of many traffic infractions, it may adversely affect your ability to obtain employment. Moreover, if you have any history of driving while under the influence, the possibility increases of your being passed over for a criminal justice position—especially if driving a work vehicle is part of the job.

Drunk or drugged driving[2] can lead to serious accidents or incidents resulting in critical injury or death. And the criminal justice profession has not been immune from such tragedy. A drunk federal agent, after waking up in the car of a fellow agent who was transporting him home, pulled his gun and shot his co-worker dead. Then there was the law enforcement officer who awoke after a night of drinking to find blood on his car's exterior. Concluding that he had killed a pedestrian, he committed suicide. (It was later determined that he had run over an animal.)

An assessment of your driving record will be used to help gauge how responsible you are and for determining whether you are eligible to operate official vehicles. In an employer's eyes, it is another valuable piece of the personality puzzle.

Life Application Exercise

What conclusions would you draw about a person whose driving record exposed three tickets for speeding in the past year—plus one for driving while intoxicated, resulting in a conviction where there was no accident involved? Would that affect your decision to hire the person even if they would not need to operate a work vehicle?

Money

The year 2011 found many Americans experiencing financial difficulties due to a severe and long-standing recession. Among those facing economic challenges are those aspiring to work in the criminal justice field. Layoffs, property foreclosures, and poor credit ratings are commonplace—and may appear to be an insurmountable disadvantage in the job application process.

---

[2] Less reported yet still a serious problem is driving while drugged. One study suggests that more than half of those admitted to trauma centers after automobile accidents test positive for illegal drugs. (Hartley, 2003)

Certainly, in reviewing your credit history, many criminal justice agencies want to ensure that you have satisfied your debts. If you pay back creditors as agreed, you send a message to prospective employers and others that you can act responsibly. The opposite impression can apply if you do not pay your bills or continuously pay them late without cause.

So how do you deal with the revelation that your credit history and current financial situation is less than perfect?

Though not as severe as the current recession, the economic downturn of 1979 was bad enough to adversely affect the results of my credit history check when I sought work as a federal agent. Upon my unexpected layoff from the Detroit Police Department, I sent letters to most of my creditors explaining my situation. I advised that I could not make payments at that time but promised to pay as soon as I was able. This took a while because my next job paid substantially less. However, eventually, one by one I was able to pay each creditor what I owed. The relief I felt with this accomplishment is hard to express; but the dignity I could maintain when proof was demanded of my having satisfied some of these debts was invaluable.

When it came time for my background investigation by the federal government, the subject of my credit came up because one of the creditors had not updated the record that I had satisfied the debt. However, having saved my payment receipts, I was able to demonstrate that I had. [3] I do not know for certain what would have happened if I had not paid these creditors, but I am glad I did not have to worry about it. If you ever find yourself in a situation where you fall on hard times, develop a plan and chip away at the debt as quickly as you are able. It will look much better than appearing to have ignored the problem.

One reason I was able to repay the creditors within a reasonable timeframe was because my debt was not substantial. Credit reports exhibiting excessive borrowing with insufficient income appear unbalanced and undisciplined; a high debt ratio is one of the most common reasons for entering into bankruptcy. The good news is that neither high debt nor insolvency alone necessarily disqualifies a person from working in the criminal justice field.

Still one must factor in what a bankruptcy, foreclosure, or any other evidence of serious financial difficulties may indicate to a prospective employer about your levels of responsibility and dependability. Regarding a bankruptcy, circumstances will be

---

[3] Maintaining your financial records can be particularly helpful if you wind up in a situation where you have to pay back debt at a slower pace than originally agreed or deal with a collection agency. Creditors may say they will remove derogatory items from your credit report once you have repaid debts, but sometimes they do not. Never rely solely on a creditor to clear your name. Keep copies of canceled checks and receipts so you can demonstrate that a particular debt was satisfied should it ever come up.

evaluated. Did the person carelessly run up debt and then bail? Was there a hardship such as loss of job or death of the family's main wage earner? Each case is viewed individually and in context, so if your intentions are honorable, even in the face of a poor credit history, you may be able to make it through this screening—just keep notes, in ready-to-submit letter form, that detail your particular situation.

Once again, if you are new to the credit world, avoid over-extension—including taking on too much college loan debt. Although tempting, borrowing more money than you need for tuitions and the bare essentials can make repayment difficult. Unlike other debt, if you default on student loans, that information will remain on your credit report and the government will aggressively seek repayment by such aggravating tactics as commandeering your income tax refund.

Two words that no one ever wants to hear relating to credit are *identity theft*. This crime carries the potential of distorting, damaging, or destroying the creditworthiness of its victims. Always take care to guard your social security number and other important financial information, because cunning criminals are constantly seeking new ways to get it. It has been estimated than 11 million people have fallen victim and billions of dollars defrauded. (BJS, 2010) Repairing the damage left by identity theft is stressful and can require a tremendous amount of energy and time—it's the reason not one criminal justice executive I know would be willing to hire a person who engages in the offense of identity theft.[4]

Aside from your credit report, a background investigation may include an examination of how you handle your checking account. Passing bad checks or excessive bouncing of checks can be interpreted as irresponsibility, while failure to pay court-ordered child support will likely be viewed as extreme irresponsibility. Additionally, any evidence of tax evasion will not likely sit well with public institutions (i.e., your prospective employer) that depend on the civic duty of paying taxes for their operating budgets.

It all boils down to personal responsibility, and your ability to convince prospective employers that you can be entrusted with a position in the criminal justice field.

Criminal History

Shoplifting is stealing! It's not a prank, a joke, or a thrill. It's a crime. Even if it's your first offense, you could be punished with up to $2,000 in fines and five or more years in prison, plus a record that could haunt you for the rest of your life. *We prosecute shoplifters. Please don't risk it!*—Wal-Mart Stores, Inc., 1997

---

[4] Except perhaps as an informant-consultant hired for a purpose to strengthen internal controls.

I observed these words on a sign inside a restroom at a Wal-Mart store. This warning communicates clearly what has been repeated throughout this book: "...a record that will haunt you for the rest of your life." Once you are arrested for anything, there is a good chance that it will remain in a system of records indefinitely. What this means is that any criminal justice employer evaluating your record will have access to the information. An arrest is accompanied by fingerprinting, which also presents a means by which your information can be accessed through a national database regardless of any name change. This fact is important because even agencies that do not require extensive background investigations at minimum will check for the existence of a criminal record.

Any arrest or conviction will be included in a criminal record. Crimes are classified as felonies or misdemeanors, with felonies being the more serious. Most criminal justice agencies refrain from hiring convicted felons except in cases of expungement or other legal justification, such as a conviction reversal on appeal.[5] But generally speaking, even one felony conviction is enough to disqualify a person from being able to obtain many criminal justice positions. So basically, arrests and convictions for the serious crimes of murder, aggravated assault, robbery, rape, grand larceny, automobile theft, or arson will preclude you from employment in the criminal justice field. Less serious felonies, and even violent misdemeanors, can automatically disqualify a candidate from becoming a law enforcement officer in the U.S.

Under the Lautenberg Amendment to the Federal Gun Control Act, it is a federal crime for law enforcement officers to possess a firearm or ammunition, including service weapons, if they have been convicted of a state misdemeanor charge of domestic violence.[6] Moreover, those seeking employment in policing should know that the law applies to convictions before and after its effective date of September 30, 1996 (U.S. Department of Justice, 1998), meaning past behavior may already restrict your employment in the criminal justice field.

Even within the range of misdemeanor crimes, some are regarded more seriously than others and may be treated as felonies for purposes of hire. For example, while

---

[5] Even an expungement is not a guarantee that records are not available to criminal justice agencies. A BJS (2003) report containing the results of policies/practices of state criminal history repositories regarding modification of felony convictions found that 24 states have statutes that provide for record expungement. However, only 11 of the states actually destroy the records. The situation is even bleaker for those attempting to conceal pardons: The same study found that while all 50 states have statutes for the granting of pardons, in 45 states and the District of Columbia, the criminal history record is retained with the action noted.

[6] Title 18, U.S.C., Section 922(g)(9).

inexpensive damage is technically classified as a misdemeanor, a malicious destruction of property conviction for a heinous act may result in disqualification. Also, crimes committed that were felonies and later pleaded down to a misdemeanor may create a suitability problem. Background investigators may consult arrest reports as well as any other information to clarify what occurred in order to reach a determination as to whether it has bearing on one's level of responsibility, judgment, or potential for future offending.

Criminal justice hopefuls must strive to behave ethically because borderline activities—as non-prescribed steroid usage did in 1988—can suddenly become illegal overnight. Moreover, law enforcement can follow trends, as happened when the music industry decided to actively seek prosecution of those illegally downloading copyrighted material. The enforcement du jour is mortgage fraud and among those charged are government officials. New laws and targeted enforcement are reasons why criminal justice candidates should strive to maintain moral upstanding in all areas of their lives. Always view your decision-making through the eyes of a potential employer.

Short of arrest, sometimes police contacts result in temporary detention for questioning followed by release. No problem, right? It depends on whether the contact was entered into a log. Some police departments, particularly those on college campuses, keep records of detentions or a notation of the police contact. Perhaps even an incident report is filed. Security officers at places of business often document incidents as well. Any of this information can be aired in a background investigation.

In addition to criminal records and recorded police contacts, unproven allegations can hinder your ability to obtain employment in the criminal justice field. Since many law enforcement agencies that conduct criminal investigations maintain internal databases for analyzing intelligence, if your name appears as one associating with criminal targets, you may lose out on a job and never know why. Other covert investigative practices involve tracing your name, license plate number, phone number, etc.

Want to know what kind of information about you is available? The Freedom of Information Act[7] provides the public with opportunity to request and receive information contained in government records. Prior to a background investigation, consider how associations and police contacts may have already affected your prospects for certain jobs. Juvenile contact with the police, including felony arrests unless you are charged as an adult, usually are exempt from release during background checks. However, if you are still a juvenile you should also avoid detention or arrest as the

---

[7] 5 U.S.C. § 552, As Amended By Public Law No. 104-231, 110 Stat. 3048. There are some restrictions on information contained in law enforcement records; the entire Act can be read at www.justice.gov.

derogatory information may come out in other ways. Friends or family or people you grew up with, for example, are often the sources for providing background investigators with details of unpleasant incidents.

Evidence of arrest or conviction is not an automatic disqualification for a criminal justice career. But all entries on a criminal record will be analyzed from various angles in the employment screening process. Most employers will overlook youthful indiscretions if there is no pattern of misconduct stretching into your adult life. But again, keep in mind that due to the volume of applications for in-demand positions, employers attempt to screen out as many people as possible. For the rare occasion when it comes down to just two candidates with all things being equal; the one without the blemish will more likely be selected. A background investigator logically starts the investigation with a criminal history check so that if there is anything seriously derogatory, a candidate can be disqualified before more time and money is expended.

Prior Work History

A background investigation obviously will entail a review of your prior work experience. Since a great deal of an employed person's waking hours is spent each day at work, interviewing coworkers and supervisors about your performance and work ethic—and even in off-site social settings such as restaurants and bars—can be quite revealing, and a source critical to evolving your composite.

Suppose a criminal record reveals a police contact for malicious destruction of property leading to a concern that a job applicant has "anger management" problems. Then, several former coworkers indicate that the candidate seemed moody much of the time—snapping at others for no apparent reason. Additionally, a supervisor notes that the applicant had been disciplined for screaming at clients. The cumulative observation from these reports shows a candidate with ill temperament. And one that is probably unsuited to work in the criminal justice field.

Most pressing for background investigators will be determining the actual circumstances under which you terminated from previous employment. If you ended one job to take a better, higher-paying one or for other valid reasons, the effect will likely be neutral. But if you were fired, a background investigator will seek to determine why. In the military, for example, it is a discharging offense to test positive for drugs. Some state or local governments prohibit those having obtained a dishonorable military discharge from obtaining firearms (BJS, 2003), which would limit hiring for sworn law enforcement positions. Being dismissed from any job for drugs, thefts, or any other integrity related reason is bad news for anyone's career.

Your prior personnel files also will be scrutinized for positive and negative references. If your original job application is in the file, it may be reviewed against any responses you have given to your prospective employer. This is why you must be honest in filling out *every* application or questionnaire—it is the best protection in ensuring that your answers remain consistent. A background investigator will take note if the personnel file demonstrates that any disciplinary action was taken, factoring the circumstances into his or her recommendation for hire. With the arrival of the Web, for example, many agencies revised their internal policies to include a prohibition for visiting sexually explicit sites while on the job. Although banned websites are often blocked, determined employees frequently find a way around the filters. Conduct such as this would be considered derogatory and highly prejudicial.

A personnel file may also include complaints lodged by clients, customers, or others with whom one may have interacted. As people sometimes complain without merit, criticism alone is not generally enough to affect hiring decisions. However, a pattern of complaints is another matter. I once reviewed a candidate who received rave reviews from most co-workers and supervisors, but not from others with whom he interacted. The pattern that emerged was one of rudeness and hostility in the applicant's prior dealings with the general public. Only one or two of these allegations were proven to have been founded; however, based upon my review of the underlying information, these complaints were quite egregious, leading to a non-recommendation. A small number of unfounded complaints should not cause any problem. But if you are on the receiving end of many complaints, you may want to weigh the reasons behind them and document them for later recall if needed.

Along with good demeanor, dependability is crucial to your employment in the criminal justice field. You are expected to be where you are required to be at the right time and doing what you are charged to do—or the consequences can be severe. Consider, for example, the prosecutor who does not appear in court to argue at a hearing and a defendant is unexpectedly released on bond. Or the officer who does not make it to a scene on schedule and a dangerous fugitive eludes capture. You must be able to accept direction, follow instruction, and discharge your duties accordingly—often without direct supervision. Therefore, anything that may have bearing on your competency is considered fair game in a background investigation.

References and Your Reputation

Character matters. Give some thought to what you want others to say about you, and then act in the ways that will ensure that they will say what you would want a prospective employer to hear.

But…what *will* they say about you? Friends, family, neighbors, landlords, college professors, and just about anybody—given the opportunity by a background investigator—may reveal whatever they know about you. Many criminal justice agencies pay a premium to investigators to find all kinds of people, both intimate and less subjective, with whom you have come into contact.

One's reputation is a peculiar thing: while you can work to improve it now for the future, at the time when critical career decisions are made about your future, your reputation is viewed as something built upon your past actions.

The essence of the prospective employer's research is determining whether you have demonstrated responsible behavior in your past. That certainly is a question posed to previous employers. Were you dependable? Were you trustworthy? Were you responsible? No employer wants to think that when the time comes for you to start work that you are going to be a problem. Again, the best way for a hiring manager to predict how you will work in the future is to check out how you worked in the past. Do not worry about isolated situations where you may have experienced a bad boss, or company officials disgruntled because you left—if you did a good job and were dependable, the truth will likely prevail when all information is reviewed. Even if there is one job where you were not as dependable as you should have been, it's the *pattern* that interests background investigators the most. Does your composite from every possible angle point to a sneaky, untrustworthy individual or a person who is honest?

All of the information background investigators collect from the many sources checked is compiled and reviewed by a succession of people from human resource specialists to security programs personnel. They will make the recommendations regarding your hire. Concerns raised by specialists are often reviewed by supervisors in increasing rank before a security clearance may be granted. If you believe that you have any issues in your past that may turn up and create problems for you during a background investigation, you should prepare answers to those issues ahead of time and be ready to respond. Gaps in employment or long periods of time when you were not in college or otherwise occupied may appear negative. Be prepared to explain what was going on during those periods.

A word of caution while we are on the subject of references: Decide carefully who you, as a reference, are willing to endorse—and think about how this may reflect upon you. If it turns out that you recommended an individual whose character, integrity, and/or performance fails to live up to your accolades, it can negatively impact your own reputation and diminish your credibility.

Chapter 15

Screenings

There are various screenings that you are likely to undergo in your quest for employment in the criminal justice field. They include: urinalysis, polygraph examination, and psychological evaluation. The purpose of the various screenings is pretty much the same as with the background investigation: your prospective employer wants to be sure that you are responsible, dependable, and trustworthy. These screenings are designed to test your honesty.

While the background investigation delves behind the scenes, without your direct participation, these screenings are either intrusive or are administered face to face—which may result in some personal discomfort. Beyond your obvious willingness to do a good job, these tests will get closer to determining your capability. For example, a psychological or physical exam can reveal limitations beyond one's control and/or knowledge that would affect one's ability to do an acceptable job.

These tests also further winnow the candidate pool. My application to become an officer with the Detroit Police Department in 1977 provides a good example. At the time, the department indicated that for every one hundred individuals who began the process of application, only ten people were actually hired following the various screenings. That was decades ago, and today we find even more candidates are likely to apply for a smaller number of jobs—making competition very stiff.

It is important to remember: Everyone must undergo the same process. During these screenings, many factors can disqualify you. Apprehension, anger, or any negative emotion displayed in the course of testing may not directly or significantly impact your scores but likely will not sit well with a prospective employer—and, in view of the number of candidates, may land you in the limbo-like category of qualified but not hired.

Testing for Drugs through Urinalysis

It is natural for most people to be anxious about intrusions into their lives. I myself had a strangely mixed reaction to my employer's decision to test the staff for the presence of drugs in the mid-1980s. On one level I felt insulted, since drug testing suggested to me distrust. But on another level, I was apprehensive. I knew that I had never used drugs, so I was not worried what such a test would reveal unless....unless the results got mixed up or something went awry with it. And if there was a problem with the test, how would I defend myself? My overactive imagination caused me to develop contingencies in my mind, including a plan to submit a specimen to an independent lab immediately after providing a sample at work.

Now, over twenty years later, I rarely give this procedure a second thought. Not only were my fears never realized,[8] I have accepted that my agency's objective was to demonstrate to the public that we took being drug-free seriously and willingly submitted to testing as a sign of our commitment. Criminal justice professionals are, after all, charged with recommending and enforcing legislation as well as prosecuting various illegal acts, and there can be no compromising these responsibilities. When people ingest drugs and become high, an alternate state of reality ensues. For employees to be expected to make sound judgments—such as, for law enforcement officers, exercising deadly force—while under the influence of mind-altering substances is unacceptable. Sobriety is necessary in discharging the very important duties of the office we are entrusted to hold.

There is another reason criminal justice agencies do not want drug-using employees. Chronic drug users pose unique threats to criminal justice agencies, especially organizations handling and housing drug evidence. Drug-using employees have been known to not only pilfer money from co-workers, but to steal drug evidence for consumption or resale. Theft of evidence jeopardizes the prosecution of a primary case and often results in prosecutors examining all of the pending (and even closed) cases of the suspect employee. The common outcome is government attorneys' refusal to bring to court those cases. Prosecutors know that such situations, along with the criminal justice professional's credibility, will be exploited by defense attorneys.

Drug use is a hot topic in American culture, debated regularly and rigorously. There are some that would move for drug legalization. Those who would favor drug legalization, however, usually do not emanate from the law enforcement community. Criminal justice professionals in general would be expected to either remain neutral on such issues or at least to maintain the status quo of existing laws. However, there

---

[8] And no, I never did get an independent test. I felt reassured when the procedure included sealing your own specimen and that there were two vials—one of which would be available for re-testing and verification if needed.

are public figures who have taken a contrary position on this issue. For example, former New Mexico Governor Gary Johnson came under fire for his push to legalize drugs after disclosing his own marijuana and cocaine use (CNN, 1999); appearing in a serious interview on the otherwise satirical television program *The Colbert Report* in 2010, Johnson continued to support the decriminalization of marijuana. Regardless of one's position on drug legalization, there are those who would rationalize that if a politician can use drugs, why can't they?

Most positions in the field of criminal justice are not political appointments,[9] which afford wider latitude in conduct and speech; hired public servant criminal justice positions are governed by standards of conduct that are higher than those of politicians. For example, while drug use can disqualify you from certain jobs, typically this is not the case for politicians. Even policy makers responsible for allowing urinalysis screening within federal law enforcement agencies and advocating these screenings in the workplace are not necessarily themselves subject to such testing. Bad acts on the part of political figures are frequently judged by constituents, who may "fire" them; but government employees usually can be dismissed for much less. So even while the debate over legalization continues, you would be wise to commit to remaining drug-free.

In addition to those who may lie about drug use, there are also those who try to beat the drug test. These attempts range from drinking herbal teas to flush drugs from bodily systems and using certain chemicals to "spike" the specimens themselves to having people thought to be drug-free providing the sample. This is not to give you advice on how to beat a test, but rather to dissuade you from trying—because there is only a small chance that you will succeed and detection will result in immediate disqualification. Even those who abstain from drug use for a period prior to a test may get caught when a sample of hair is examined. Besides that, random testing can reveal ongoing usage and a user could wind up losing the job anyway.[10]

Dismissing drug use as "experimentation" depends on timing and number of times. If it occurred while you were in high school or middle school, it will likely be viewed very differently by a prospective employer than if it happened in your junior year of college as a CRJ major. Past drug use at any point in your life is likely to be

---

[9] Some criminal justice professionals obtain their positions through elections or appointments from a government leader—such as a president or governor. Such positions include county sheriffs and federal agency heads.

[10] Different drugs can be detected in one's urine for varying periods of time. Marijuana, for example, is detectable substantially longer than cocaine and heroin. However, most drugs are detected in hair samples for much longer periods than in urine. More information about workplace drug testing is available from the Department of Labor's website at www.dol.gov.

a sensitive subject for you, particularly since you will be required to disclose the type and extent of your use[11] along with a urine sample. The purpose of a urinalysis screening test is to detect those who are *currently* using drugs and deny them employment.

The best advice: If you have never used drugs and you are a CRJ major, for the sake of your intended career, do not start now! [12]

The Polygraph Exam

I would venture a bet that if I asked candidates which part of the screening process frightens them the most, it would be the polygraph examination. Submitting to a polygraph exam may feel even more uncomfortable than submitting to a urinalysis screening.

Perhaps you have never thought of submitting to a polygraph exam and have difficulty believing its reputation to scare people. Well, consider this: When some law enforcement recruiters mention during orientation sessions that a polygraph examination is required, the pool of candidates immediately shrinks. I learned from one executive who monitors and enforces police standards in his state that it is not unusual to begin a law enforcement orientation session for new applicants with 500 individuals…and, after advising the candidates about the statewide requirement of a polygraph exam, seeing only about 150 individuals return after a break.

Not every criminal justice employer uses polygraph exams for screening applicants.[13] But based on a perceived benefit of confirming candidates' honesty about their responses during the application process, the trend is that more of them—especially in the course of filling sensitive positions—are doing so. Agencies cannot spring a polygraph exam on you; as an applicant, you are entitled to a written notice before testing. (Department of Labor, 1988) In addition to its use as a screening device for employment, polygraph tests are administered by some criminal justice agencies for certain positions throughout one's career either routinely or for a specific purpose.

---

[11] For example, the U.S. Drug Enforcement Administration includes a drug questionnaire on job vacancy websites. The questionnaire is very intrusive and requires applicants to disclose the types of substances they have tried, and when. Moreover, candidates must certify that their answers are truthful: the form asserts that "misstatement of fact or omission of information" may subject the candidate to disqualification from further consideration for hire.

[12] Besides, drugs are just plain nasty. For more convincing, check out Appendix C: "Don't Eat Crap and Die (The Sobering Facts about Street Drugs)."

[13] While the Employee Polygraph Protection Act prohibits most private employers from using the lie detector tests before or during employment, federal, state, and local governments are exempt from this law. (U.S. Department of Labor, 1988)

During various periods, some federal agencies have employed the use of polygraphs to root out spies and other corrupt persons. For example, the arrest and pending internal investigation of large numbers of border patrol agents led Congress to pass the Anti-border Corruption Act of 2010.[14] With a goal of fostering integrity, the Act calls for the Secretary of Homeland Security to ensure that U.S. Customs and Border Protection (CBP) law enforcement applicants receive a polygraph before being offered employment. It also requires the CBP to give polygraphs to existing employees. (Yager, 2011)

Those expecting to undergo a polygraph exam probably experience unease on many levels. Without any intention whatsoever to deceive, you may wonder whether you can trust the results produced by the machine and/or the examiner. The primary purpose of the polygraph exam is to ascertain if the information you have included in your previous written and oral statements is accurately represented. You can obtain hints about what will be asked by reviewing your application and other related documents such as the Standard Form 86[15] if you are seeking federal employment. If you can regard the polygraph exam as confirming everything you have already stated—particularly about sensitive topics such as past drug use or criminal behavior—it may alleviate your anxiety. Basically, it is just another phase of the application process.

Interviews

Interviews can be as much of a screening mechanism as any other part of the process. For our purposes, I just want to reiterate the importance of being truthful in your responses, as the consistency of what you say during your interview will be checked during other stages of the process. Recognizing that screenings are expensive endeavors, do not be surprised if interviewers ask some of the tough questions up front—as doing so affords an opportunity to screen out undesirable candidates as quickly as possible. Remember, it is worse to be caught in a lie than it is to reveal something uncomfortable or embarrassing. And bear in mind that some agencies may already have the answers to questions posed. Moreover, knowing the reasons why you are seeking a particular position of trust is advantageous. You can usually provide superior responses by having researched the job and its challenges thoroughly so that you can convincingly articulate your interest and dedication.

---

[14] Bill S.3243 can be viewed at www.gpo.gov. The Anti-border Corruption Act of 2010 was signed into law by President Obama on January 4, 2011. www.whitehouse.gov

[15] The lengthy Standard Form 86, "Questionnaire for National Security Positions," is accessible at www.opm.gov.

The DOs

There are many proactive and common sense steps you can take to prepare for a background investigation and frame your experience in the most favorable light. A few of these follow:

Consider volunteering for community service. Such work demonstrates selflessness and a genuine interest in contributing to the greater good. Including volunteer efforts on your resume will help a prospective employer evaluate your character. Uncompensated internships can also give you a jump on developing skills that will be key to your career in criminal justice.

Work as hard as you possibly can in your current job and during coursework. Be professional while discharging your duties, school assignments, and conducting work-related social interactions; develop your reputation as someone who is competent *and* polite. Awards, accolades, and other recognitions look impressive on applications and resumes—so strive for them. Make it easy for your professional references to be enthusiastic about you.

Avoid "shortcuts." Those who try to circumvent details and extended focus on the job may find themselves with a hobbled work ethic. Do not ignore the fine points and the need for analysis, especially in the criminal justice field.

Avoid all drug use and experimentation. If you have never experimented with drugs in your life—please do not start now. If you have never done drugs, commend yourself and vow never to bow to this temptation.

Foster self-control. Do not give in to temper tantrums, spontaneous outbursts, or other extreme behavior. An inability to maintain self-control is neither productive nor reputation-bolstering, and it will not build others' confidence in you.

Go light on alcohol consumption. Alcoholic beverages can lower your inhibitions to such an extent that you may do or say things that you may regret later. The extent of your regular alcohol consumption and how you handle yourself when drinking may become issues in the course of any background examination.

A discussion based on this material can enhance your understanding of the intrusions that accompany the selection process. Use the following questions to review what you have learned:

1.) Why are background investigations conducted? Why would the particular criminal justice agency in which you are seeking employment need to pursue such checks?

2.) If you were a criminal justice executive, what would be some factors you would take into consideration when ordering background investigations?

3.) Do you believe that urinalysis screening for the presence of drugs and polygraph examinations are necessary procedures? Why or why not?

While some of these guidelines in this part of the book may seem arbitrary or moralistic, please bear in mind that I am offering them as a professional who has worked in the criminal justice field and been involved in all phases of the federal hiring process from interviews to administering the oath of office. Some readers may conclude that portions of the advice offered in this section are "unfair"—and you may have some good points to argue. But what is the advantage of pursuing a career that you suspect will offensively violate privacy or may not be attainable based on your personal history? Save your time, effort, and money, and consider this a reality check.

Part IV

You Got It!
Now Keep It!

Chapter 16

Beyond the Hiring Process: Keeping It Together

After all it has taken you to get that fantastic criminal justice position, the hardest part is over…right? Not so fast. To paraphrase an old saying, the same thing it took to get the job is the same thing it takes to keep it. Earning entry into the criminal justice field is partly a function of your having demonstrated reasonably high values and morals to this point in your life. Keeping and advancing your career requires the same commitment to making good decisions, exercising sound judgment, and behaving the right way.

This all sounds pretty easy, but the stakes are high. Anyone who has been in law enforcement for a number of years will tell you that no matter how good you are or how hard you work or how dedicated you are, all it takes is one poor decision to de-rail your career—whether it involves corruption, discrimination, or abuse of power.[1] It is sobering that many who find themselves mired in such an unfortunate situation do not know precisely how they wound up there.

I know of no one who deliberately decides to become corrupt or unethical. In many cases, it is a gradual decline in self-discipline and character. It can happen to anyone who is not careful. How many times have you found yourself mindlessly doing something that you did not mean to do? Or falling in with a group of friends who were just a little too "fun?" Maintaining an ethical criminal justice career requires not only periodic self-examination, but discussion and cross-checking among professionals in the field. There

---

[1] While still relatively rare, each year law enforcement officers are removed from their positions. The FBI's study of 107 agents who were dismissed, resigned, or retired while under investigation for criminal and serious misconduct between 1986 and 1999 found less than one agent per thousand was dismissed. (*Federal Employees News Digest,* 2004) On the other hand, the high numbers of U.S. Customs and Border Protection employees arrested or under investigation for corruption circa 2010 was substantial enough to increase congressional oversight. (Yager, 2011)

will always be talk about, followed by the practice of, doing the right thing. It begins with providing a framework for facilitating a healthy mindset—one that will help you sustain an ethical criminal justice career.

Life Application Exercise #1

After sixteen years on the run, in 2011 the infamous James "Whitey" Bulger, a reputed mobster, was captured. Contemporaneous with his alleged murdering and drug dealing, Bulger was a long-time FBI informant—a relationship that is blamed for his ability to flee as well as the corruption of several FBI agents. In Florida, one former agent was convicted of second degree murder in 2008 for his association with Bulger in a mob hit. The Bulger case continues to cast suspicion on the agency with rampant speculation that Bulger may act as an informant against other corrupt agents who have since retired.

Here's the thing: If federal agents are convicted of corrupt behavior occurring when they were employed, their pensions can be revoked. Moreover, two U.S. Senators (Mark Kirk and Richard Blumenthal) are introducing legislation to expand the Pension Revocation Law for Congressional members involved in violations of trust after retirement. Do you believe it is fair for employees to lose their pensions if corruption is later detected? Should the fact that they engaged in otherwise stellar careers and retired in good standing have any bearing? Do you believe those engaging in misconduct occurring post-retirement should have their pensions subject to revocation?

Life Application Exercise #2

A controversial ATF operation dubbed "too fast too furious" is the subject of ongoing Congressional inquiry. The venture encouraged gun dealers to sell firearms to suspected drug traffickers including Mexican nationals. The investigation of at least one murder—that of a border patrol agent—traced the weapon used back to the operation. This and the fact that other guns were discovered at crime scenes resulted in the operation's suspension and sparked outrage that such a risky technique was unleashed. While it appears that ATF and its parent agency, the DOJ, believed their attempts to identify drug cartel members by this method would yield positive results, the plan was clearly flawed.

Do you believe Congress should continue to press to identify all personnel responsible for proposing and approving the operation? What, if any, action do you think should be imposed for personnel directly involved in approving the operation? What, if any, action do you think should be imposed for personnel *executing* the operation, but not approving?

Chapter 17

Deciding to Do the Right Thing

Some time ago, I heard a provocative advertising tagline on the radio. It went something like this: "Be good, but if you cannot, be careful." This statement seems permissive on the point of doing wrong. In other words, if one chooses to do wrong, just be careful while you doing it—and do not get hurt or caught. Perhaps my taking offense at the ad's potentially destructive inference has more to do with my concern for a society that at times overlooks opportunities to do something positive.

Before attempting to comprehend any specific standards for right and wrong in the criminal justice field, you must be secure in the ethical foundation of your own life. If you build a solid ethical base, every decision you make is likely to be well within the standards of conduct for any criminal justice position.[2] Your aim should be that every decision you make be on the right side of "right."

Ethics is conforming to the right standards of conduct for a given profession. The emphasis is on the word "right." Arguably, the "right standards of conduct" for the criminal justice profession are higher than for most other fields—some believe too high. I have occasionally heard complaints from colleagues and subordinates that did not know when they were doing something wrong. However, I believe that we almost instinctively know when we are doing something right or wrong. I do concede that there are those whose consciences, for whatever reason, have become so warped or damaged that they can longer distinguish between right and wrong.

---

[2] Even when your criminal justice position requires unusual or challenging assignments, such as undercover work, you can still remain ethical. I once had a debate with a member of the clergy whose perception of undercover work was that it was deceptive and wrong. There is no ambivalence within me relative to such work; I view it as necessary to conduct certain types of investigations in the pursuit of justice.

For most, determining the difference is simple. Start by asking yourself, *Is my impending action something of which I should be proud or ashamed?* Certain physiological or psychological responses are indicative of right (e.g. elation, pride) or wrong (e.g. sadness, shame) behavior. Various internal feelings can cue you to the nature of a given behavior. In short, if you feel that you have done or about to do something that is right, you will feel good about it; the converse is also true. Certain external reactions can provide supporting information as to whether a decision and subsequent action was right or wrong.

The motive behind what you do is just as important. If a case or assignment takes a turn for the worse, it is not unusual for criminal justice professionals to be second-guessed and their motives questioned. One's primary defense for surviving such scrutiny is the belief that one has done the right thing and for the right reason. Developing a "moral compass" and keeping it tuned will help keep you out of trouble and bolster your defense when needed.

Some situations and scenarios which at first appear innocuous can actually cause major grief. Endeavoring to familiarize yourself with the latest cons, whether by utilizing the Internet or by paying attention to the nightly news, can not only save you from financial losses but heartache, embarrassment, and professional repercussions.

Early in my career, I was approached by seemingly respectable people to join a pyramid scheme. At the time, I didn't know the name for this type of activity, but I knew instinctively that it did not seem right. In particular, I found it objectionable that I would receive monies from others who I would need to hassle into "investing," who in turn would have to hassle others. Many years later, in 2010, I learned I had averted another scam involving a Ponzi schemer who preyed on criminal justice practitioners and then committed suicide as his victims learned they were collectively defrauded of millions in savings. The ensuing investigation revealed that the charismatic crook lured unsuspecting victims with promises of exclusivity to purchase non-existent secret bond funds.

Criminal justice professionals are held to higher ethical standards and are expected to be "smarter" and more aware. It may be a harsh reality, but those in the field who find themselves entangled in cons and schemes—whether as a "mark" (victim) or perpetrator—are often discredited and rarely forgiven.

Life Application Exercise #1

This is an exercise about right and wrong that I use in ethics workshops. It involves the facilitator breaking a class into groups consisting of three or more persons that confer privately to discuss the following:

• Group #1 develops a list of ways in which people react internally when they perceive that they have done something right.

• Group #2 develops a list of ways in which people react externally when they perceive that they have done something right.

• Group #3 develops a list of ways in with people react internally when they perceive that they have done something wrong.

 • Group #4 develops a list of ways that people react externally when they perceive that they have done something wrong.

• Group #5 is to answer the question: If no one knows about a job applicant or practitioner's particular behavior, does it have the potential to influence decision-making or conduct? Support the answer with examples.

• Group #6 is to answer the question: If everyone knows about a job applicant or practitioner's particular behavior, does it have the potential to influence decision-making or conduct? Support the answer with examples.

• Group #7: Recognizing that ethics is conforming to the highest standards of conduct for a given profession, create a list of principles that you feel are ethically right for a position you are considering.

• Group #8: Recognizing that ethics is conforming to the highest standards of conduct for a given profession, list some actions or approaches that you feel would be wrong for a criminal justice position you are considering.

When the workshop reassembles, each group should elect a spokesperson. The facilitator should have each spokesperson summarize the results of the group conferences for general discussion.

For this exercise, I have found the responses to be uniform from workshop to workshop—with the consensus being that we all have a strong sense of the difference between right and wrong. Most of the feelings and behaviors broached in the group conferences can be categorized under "head," "heart," and "gut."

Life Application Exercise #2

This exercise involves an ethical dilemma based on a real-life situation in Brooklyn, New York involving law enforcement officers that resulted in negative publicity for their department. (Morrison, 2000)

In an effort to reduce the availability of illegal weapons, a campaign was launched by a criminal justice agency to purchase guns from the public. At some point, it was discovered that one-third of the weapons surrendered for cash came from law enforcement officers—including one of the highest-ranking members of the department.

Additional information indicated that the officers were motivated to do this because they had obtained new guns, rendering their old duty weapons obsolete.[3] Moreover, the officers had purchased the swapped weapons with their own money.

Although this was a "no questions asked" program, its administrators later posted signs making it clear that the officers' weapons were ineligible for exchange—and this was reported by local media in the hopes that the situation would not be repeated. Ask yourself the following questions:

1.) Was the officers' conduct more right or more wrong?

2.) If the officers knew their actions would result in media attention, do you believe they would still have exchanged the guns for money?

3.) Does the fact that officers paid for the old weapons they exchanged have any bearing on your opinion versus if these weapons had been paid for by the department?

---

[3] Beginning in the late 1980s, many police departments shifted from revolvers to semi-automatic handguns as duty weapons.

4.) Cash-for-weapons programs are frequently co-sponsored by another entity, such as city council. How do you think the police department looked to the public they served during this time?

5.) Prepare a mock "comment" for posting on the news story reporting this controversy.

6.) How do you think this situation should have been handled both internally and publicly by the law enforcement agency?

I have facilitated lively group discussions with several criminal justice professionals using this exercise. The most commonly weighed mitigating circumstance has been the fact that the officers used their own money to purchase the guns—leading many discussion participants to regard the officers' unexpected participation in the weapons exchange program less harshly. Still, the overriding conclusion of these sessions has been that the *intent* of the program—i.e. to help clear the streets of *illegal* weapons— meant that the officers should not have swapped their guns for cash.

Chapter 18
Rules, Rules, Rules

The criminal justice field encompasses a variety of positions, each with its own set of documents guiding employee conduct. There are, to be sure, many overlapping standards, and the Department of Justice (DOJ) is among employers that includes a multitude of them in its Standards of Conduct for its employees. These standards govern thousands of people, with some extending even to contractors and vendors who do business with the department. For example, all DOJ employees are expected to avoid situations wherein personal interests conflict with the best interests of the government. To ensure that this does not happen, strict guidelines are provided to DOJ employees for personal business practices to ensure that private enterprises do not conflict with government business. (DOJ, 2011)

An examination of just about any criminal justice code of ethics will reveal limitations or restrictions on how much business involvement employees many have with private entities that also engage in business with the employing agency. These are generally referred to as "conflict of interest" dealings. It is logical that conflict of interest clauses are crucial in ensuring that governmental agencies gain public confidence regarding objectivity.

The federal government employs a large number of criminal justice professionals in all of its branches.[4] Conduct rules for federal employees are relatively strict; they include a requirement to satisfy just debts and to notify co-workers before recording conversations with them. There are also statutory prohibitions. One is the restriction

---

[4] Employers in the executive branch include many agencies such as the FBI, DEA, and Alcohol, Tobacco, and Firearms. The legislative branch includes lawmakers such as Congressional representatives, while the judicial branch includes judges.

on federal employees' personal use of official vehicles[5]; if unauthorized use—even something as seemingly innocuous as stopping off at a daycare center to pick up your child—occurs, there is a mandatory 30-day suspension.

Some government positions come with extraordinary ethically based restrictions. For example, employees cannot benefit from actions taken in the course of their official duties, like purchasing seized vehicles at government auctions.[6] And depending on the position, DOJ places a one- to two-year freeze on the hiring of its former employees by any company with which it had a business relationship prior to that employee's departure.

One of the biggest catchalls on rules is "conduct unbecoming." The same behavior that may be regarded as amusing, tacky, or unseemly in your leisure time can get you disciplined or dismissed in your criminal justice role. And unbecoming conduct can be censored whether it occurs on or off duty. A general statutory conduct rule states that federal employees "shall not engage in criminal, infamous, dishonest, immoral, or notoriously disgraceful conduct, or other conduct prejudicial to the government."[7] (I was required to certify in writing my knowledge of this prohibition.)

In addition to keeping your moral compass in good working order, it is important to familiarize yourself with the standards of conduct that apply to your particular position so that you do not inadvertently violate them. Criminal justice employers have the latitude to impose a circumstance-based discipline; punishment can range from oral reprimand to dismissal. So be careful.

Life Application Exercise #1

Keeping in mind that criminal justice professionals are held to higher ethical standards, identify whether you would consider the following actions or behaviors conduct unbecoming. Try to view them from the standpoint of a criminal justice manager—so "should" will play a part in your thinking or discussion.

1.) In the office building cafeteria, an employee yells at the cashier because she takes too long to ring up the order.

---

[5] 41 CFR 101-6.4 (NIH, 2002)

[6] This prohibition generally extends to immediate family as well. For a closer examination of the ethical concerns raised by seized assets, see Appendix D, "Use Seized Monies for Treatment."

[7] 5 CFR 735.203 (Daniel, 2003)

2.) Reading a coworker's personal mail which was already open and in plain view.

3.) Spreading a story about the boss that seems to be untrue.

4.) Having an extramarital sexual relationship.

5.) Unmarried, but cohabitating.

6.) Not paying bills.

7.) Snatching identification from the hand of a person who has initially permitted you to examine it.

You probably figured out that each of the above could be construed as conduct unbecoming a criminal justice professional. The purpose of the exercise is to assist you in your critical thinking about behavior that you perhaps previously thought was no big deal. Consider that action #7 actually occurred in the State of Florida between an off-duty officer of one agency who was stopped by a deputy from another agency. Caught on tape, this confrontation escalated into an argument and struggle, and the off-duty officer was arrested. [8] It received national media attention and became an embarrassment to the entire law enforcement community; worse, it shook public confidence in the profession. Of course, this is not the only example of how situations can spin out of control when cooler heads do not prevail.

A disciplinary record also is usually factored in when decisions are being made about sanctions. If you are ever charged administratively,[9] being truthful can save you from future woes such as being deemed a non-credible witness in forthcoming court appearances—a ruling that can jeopardize your employment.

Some may consider the constrictive rules on practitioner conduct an Achilles heel. This can be a problem when someone you previously considered to be in your corner, such as an ex-spouse, suddenly is no longer there. Former intimates can disclose

---

[8] The "gone viral" video clip is accessible on the Web using the key words: "Trooper vs. Undercover Cop.

[9] Unlike in criminal cases, where those accused are entitled to remain silent, many criminal justice agencies compel employees to "talk" relative to administrative matters during internal investigations.

secrets that can undo one's career—another reason to walk the straight and narrow at all times. Protect yourself: Study the code of ethics or principles of conduct provided to you by your employer. Do not give anyone an opportunity to speak ill of you.

Life Application Exercise #2

A detective intends to retire within the next two years. Afterward, he plans to work in the private sector using skills and contacts he has made during his law enforcement career. In furtherance of his goal, the detective presently begins being especially nice to possible future employers. The owner of Company X, has been dangling a post-retirement job prospect, so the detective gives preference to Company X's services over those of others. Additionally, the detective calls other detectives whose responsibility it is to coordinate the same services in their respective field sectors—and starts bad-mouthing competing companies, suggesting he has found Company X's services to be superior. When the detective retires, he starts working for Company X.

Did the detective do anything wrong? Is this a conflict of interest?

Chapter 19

Do Criminal Justice Professionals Have Freedom of Speech?

How free your speech remains after you become a criminal justice professional is debatable. While the U.S. Constitution gives every citizen the right to freedom of speech, you may be asked to give up some of this right upon accepting employment in the criminal justice field. Agencies in this line of work cannot, for example, afford to permit employees to disclose confidential information "at will."

At the very least, agencies expect that anything you say in public will not convey a position contrary to the organization's missions and goals. Consider the following scenario:

> ...a Billings [Montana] man at the center of a national debate over freedom of speech...was convicted of felony possession of a half-gram of psilocybin mushrooms and was sentenced to three years of probation. His conviction prompted an interest in drug reform laws and he organized a Billings chapter of the National Organization for the Reform of Marijuana Laws, or NORML. He planned a concert to "raise money for an initiative to place the legalization of medicinal marijuana on the 2004 ballot....A story about the concern appeared in *The Gazette*...Three days later [the man] lost his job.... (Fitzgerald, 2003)

The man at the center of this situation insisted he was fired because of his beliefs while the employer maintained that he was not. But here's a certainty: When your ideology conflicts with your agency's mission and you speak out to the press about it, there is bound to be trouble. No matter how accurate your statements, public criticism of your employer will never be welcomed. Soldiers serving in the Iraqi war, for example, faced discipline as a result of negative statements they made about the Secretary of Defense's alleged repeated reneging on a promise to permit their return home. In response to this "grumbling and whining" to reporters, some military officials pursued charges of insubordination. (Friedman, 2003)

Your employer generally expects that you will not profit from releasing proprietary or confidential information obtained while discharging your official duties. For example, federal "employees shall not engage in financial transactions using non-public information, or allow the improper use of non-public information to further any private interests" (Daniel, 2003). This was the ethical standard under which I performed in writing the first and current editions of this book. (Obviously, I have access to much information not known or available to the general public, but it has not been included here.)

The higher a case's profile, the more eagerly information is likely to be sought. The public's thirst for more details, understandably, is always there—as it was at the time of the panic-causing serial sniper killings in Maryland and Virginia in 2002. Former Montgomery County Police Chief Charles Moose, a very public figure during the shootings, decided to write a book about the case even before the trials commenced. In response, the Montgomery County Ethics Commission forbade Chief Moose from telling his story in movie or book form before the trials. It was asserted that Chief Moose was attempting to profit from the prestige of his office. (*American Police Beat*, 2003) Chief Moose resigned shortly after this ruling.[10]

---

[10] Chief Moose's book on the sniper case, *Three Weeks in October,* was published in 2003.

Life Application Exercise

Refer back to the story about the Montana man who lost his job after there were newspaper accounts about his drug conviction and subsequent press about his efforts to get legislation passed on drug legalization. The employee was quoted as stating that he "couldn't pass the background check, they never put the application in.... I became a liability because of my political beliefs." Recognizing that beliefs affect behavior, do you feel that those holding certain beliefs should refrain from working in particular jobs where their ideology may conflict with the agency's goals and objectives? The private industry employer was quoted as saying, "What people do when they're off the job is their business." However, if the offender was a criminal justice professional, would this situation have been his employer's "business?" Would his firing based on information obtained from the press have been justified?

Chapter 20

Competency

Do you believe that how well someone is able to do their job is, or should be, a question of ethics? Is there a minimum performance threshold that should be used in deciding if a criminal justice professional should continue in the field?

Having been both a police academy trainee and an instructor, I developed a framework for pondering these questions personally and as a Life Exercise while conducting ethics workshops. The academy is the gateway for many law enforcement positions—a setting for staff to gauge an individual's aptitude, skills, and abilities from many vantage points—and it convinced me to regard competency assessment as an issue worthy of review throughout one's criminal justice career.

As an academy instructor, I endeavored to understand how recruits "washed-out" during this crucial precondition of employment. I observed that, in general, low performance is often a product of a person's *unwillingness* or *inability* to improve. When someone *will not* do what is required, it may be due to an attitude problem or an attempt to disguise incompetence. However, competency questions may also arise when someone simply *cannot* perform.

Everyone was not meant to do everything. And sometimes no matter how hard a person tries, performing the duties of a criminal justice practitioner at an acceptable level is impossible. I have greater empathy for the person who honestly cannot do a job than one who will not do it. The individual with the attitude problem has the power to change, whereas, the person who cannot perform may be hindered by physical, intellectual, or other limitations. It is always unfortunate to see a person with skills, or the potential to develop them, take those abilities for granted while there is someone else who has the right attitude but will never attain them.

We must all learn when to say "when." Sincere self-examination can reveal in-competence to an individual long before an external examination. If it is determined that you are incapable of performing duties (especially where safety or security is at issue), ethics and integrity dictate surrendering the position. Resignation is usually more advantageous than being fired.[11]

Assuming that those who cannot perform well in a criminal justice position are in the minority, we can agree that much of competency has to do with employees simply applying themselves—i.e. doing their jobs. Years ago, when I was conducting research on violence directed at witnesses, I came across a shocking example. A woman had agreed to cooperate with the D.A.'s office in the investigation of her boyfriend. The letter outlining her plea agreement was mistakenly addressed to and mailed to her boyfriend. Shortly after he obtained it, he shot her, but she survived. This illustrates how important it is for those working in the criminal justice field at every level to maintain attentiveness to detail. It can literally mean life or death.

Life Application Exercise #1

It is not uncommon when mistakes on the part of criminal justice profes-sionals becomes public and known to family or friends either by news account or personal experience that you are confronted. It's an occupational hazard that if you are one of "them," you must at least be able to provide some deeper insight into the behavior, such as a ticket or search warrant vaguely written. In fact, often people outside the profession seek inside information on the best way to prevail in court. When you are faced with these "inquests," what is your normal response? Do you typically automatically come to the defense of family or friends and give them the advice they seek? Or do you openly refuse to assist others in exploiting mistakes? Do you instead feign ignorance, secretly keeping your opinion to yourself? What is the benefit of adopting either of these positions?

---

[11] A resignation on your record is preferable to a firing when you are seeking other employment. Just because you are unable to do one job does not mean that you cannot do another. I have seen many cases where people starting out in law enforcement positions change careers within the same agency for jobs just as rewarding and with comparative pay.

Life Application Exercise #2

Suppose you are responsible for making a decision about retaining an employee. Up until recently, the worker's performance was stellar. However, after being hit in the head by a golf ball while off-duty, the paralegal now experiences difficulty concentrating and processing thoughts essential to analyzing cases. Two distinct camps have formed in the office with as many recommending the paralegal's forced disability as those calling for his retention of the same position – no matter what. Can you make a decision about the paralegal's fate based on the information supplied? What other facts would you need to decide if he should be compelled to retire or remain in his current position?

Life Application Exercise #3

Merriam-Webster defines competency as "the quality or state of being functionally adequate."[12] I hold the view that it is impossible to be functionally adequate if one is asleep. Do you agree or disagree? Debate the 2011 controversy of the sleep-on-the job air traffic controllers who missed communications from arriving flights forcing the pilots to land on their own. Should the employees have been suspended or dismissed? Would your discipline be more stringent for the controller who premeditated his actions by bringing a blanket for the makeshift bed he slept on? What do you believe led to the resignation of the Federal Aviation Administration's (FAA) head of the Air Traffic Organization?

---

[12] mw1.merriam-webster.com.

Chapter 21
Abuse of Power

Do you know someone who, when temporarily placed in charge, tends to let the position "go to his/her head?" With such a person at the helm, chaos can emerge from even a relatively stable situation. When decisions are made amid a stew of selfish motives and immature impulses, they are not likely to be in the best interests of the organization or the individuals the organization is expected to serve or protect.

Consider that law enforcement and related occupations may place entry-level personnel in positions that exercise substantial authority—wherein one's decisions and actions can have repercussions on many people for a long time. It is a tremendous responsibility requiring discipline and discretion in the discharging of duties.

Equality
A discussion of ethical behavior cannot overlook the sensitive subjects of racism, sexism, and EEO (equal employment opportunity). Treating others fairly and equitably without regard to race, ethnicity, gender, religion, sexual orientation, age, or other non-behavioral characteristics should be a goal for all criminal justice professionals. Not only is discrimination an ethical issue, it is frequently a legal issue. Equality or the perceived lack thereof also is a foundational issue: Many police/community relations problems (e.g. racial profiling, and excessive force) can be tied to it.

Behaving ethically in this area begins with admitting that there is a problem. A stubborn, even willful ignorance both in public and in the workplace has resulted in struggle for many minority and underprivileged segments of society. With such groups placing an emphasis on "fighting" for rights, it is not hard to see how parts of the criminal justice system may seem at odds with their aims both within the field and beyond it. When asked, most criminal justice professionals will advise you that they are not prejudiced—yet evidence to the contrary often is all too apparent. In fact, some who engage in discriminatory practices may not even realize it.

When I was a supervisor, an employee told me of his excitement about working with a newcomer from another agency because of that person's ethnic background. Basically, he believed that the person would be in a unique position to assist us with cases involving individuals of the same ethnicity—particularly in the translation of language and cultural idiosyncrasies. This worker went on tell me that he was also concerned that this new team member's ethnic background was one predisposed to crime. So, in order to ease his concern, he asked me if a special check on the newcomer could be arranged.

This was a glaringly discriminatory proposal. But I played along with it initially with the hope that the dialogue would become illuminating. "Well," I said, "there will be other people that you will work with from other agencies—would you like for me to do additional checks on them as well?" He said, "No, no, just this person." I reminded him that the newcomer worked for another agency where a thorough background check would have been performed. He responded: "But you know he is one of *those* people. They are not to be trusted." Recognizing that this bewildered employee did not see his request as improper, I explained the reasons I could not do as he asked. While I held the authority to exercise discretion in requesting additional background information from a parent agency, doing so purely for ethnic reasons was not only unwise, but illegal.

Sometimes people discriminate casually or unconsciously without realizing that their actions are wrong or illegal. Therefore, it is imperative that training is presented in a manner that sensitizes individuals to biases and identifies what constitutes discrimination. You will likely receive such training from your employer, but even if you do not, you should "self-train." Study the laws, practices, and policies within your agency's purview and commit to their application consistently and fairly without regard to characteristics protected under EEO laws. Moreover, examining yourself for individual bias will help you tremendously in identifying the areas within yourself that need work.

Many civil servants are given wide discretion in discharging certain duties. Law enforcement officers can use their discretion in deciding whether a misdemeanor warrants a traffic ticket or an arrest. Probation and parole officers can exercise discretion in weighing whether an individual is fit to continue living freely or should be returned to prison. Favoring one group over another when exercising discretion is not only improper, it can be very detrimental. For example, the poor and/or inconsistent use of discretion that led to the failure of many criminal justice practitioners to identify or deal with the parole violations of Phillip Garrido—a convicted sex offender—undoubtedly aggravated the plight of childhood kidnapping victim Jaycee Dugard, who Garrido and his wife Nancy Garrido held captive in California for 18 years.[13]

A prohibited extension of discretion that has the potential of being carried to extremes, racial profiling—defined as stopping a person based solely on race or ethnicity instead of an individualized suspicion arising from behavior (BJS, 2001)—has become a controversial issue in law enforcement. Yet the practice has existed, mostly quietly, for a long time. It was not until the late 1990s, when several critical incidents raised national awareness. One of them involved the shooting and wounding of unarmed minority college students during a traffic stop on the New Jersey Turnpike. It later came to light that the students were stopped because troopers were informed by supervisors that minorities were more likely to be involved in drug trafficking. (Public Agenda Online, 2002) In addition to being subject to federal monitoring and $12.9 million in damages to the victims in this case, the police department's reputation took a powerful hit.

New policies have been written and implemented throughout the criminal justice system providing guidance to employees for avoiding this illegal practice, particularly in the aftermath of the terrorist attacks on September 11, 2001. But guidance is only that, and America depends on the discretion of those criminal justice professionals making the actual contact with citizens to be sure that such contact is devoid of all inequality.[14]

Diversity training where professionals are sensitized to different cultures can improve performance and reduce incidences of excessive force. Police brutality, a topic often broached from the standpoint of discrimination, is another form of abuse of authority. It has been a frequent complaint by minorities in the U.S.—and it has

---

[13] For more on the opportunities missed by criminal justice practitioners in detecting Dugard and her children fathered by Garrido until their discovery in 2009, see the special report titled "The California Department of Corrections and Rehabilitation's Supervision of Parolee Phillip Garrido" (accessible via PDF file at www.oig.ca.gov).

[14] Criminal justice professionals other than police can initiate contacts with the public inappropriately. In my role as a law enforcement officer, I have been challenged by others in my profession based simply because of my being an African-American. In one instance, I was in a courtroom guarding persons under arrest. When the defendants were ordered to rise, the magistrate looked at me and asked if I understood his order for defendants to rise. A colleague explained to the court official (someone I held in high regard) that I was not a defendant. Another situation occurred as I traversed a courthouse area during bail hearings. One of the prosecutors, assuming I was there to seek release for a friend or family member, asked me to identify my significant other among the defendants. My point is that even well-meaning people can make snap decisions based on physical characteristics instead of behavior; most of us could improve in this area.

been substantiated in court cases that minorities have disproportionately been sub-
jected to excessive force. Some police departments have been scandalized by the actions of their officers. One city, New York paid out $16.3 million to settle 25 civil
cases involving brutality or other wrongdoing from 1994 to 2001. (McCoy, 2000)
Fortunately, we have made positive strides in this area. No longer sweeping such situations under the rug, police departments are less inclined to hire or retain officers
that engage in excessive force.

A lesson to be learned from scandals involving inequality is that individuals who
engage in illegal discrimination not only make their lives difficult but imperil their
agencies. More importantly, the very lives of co-workers can depend on facing prej-
udices. The actionable lesson for the criminal justice professional is that humans hold
biases that can often be overcome by self- examination.[15]

Unethical Behavior and the Code of Silence

Unethical acts thrive under certain conditions—like silence. When a reaction to
misbehavior is hushed, an "all clear" message is sent to the wrongdoer. Under such
circumstances, misconduct is likely to increase. Never underestimate what can happen
when an agency's culture deliberately overlooks widespread corruption. Lacking vig-
ilance and resolve, or simply fearful of the consequences of "informing" on coworkers, some employees settle for adapting to corrupt environments.

It is appalling that "the code of silence" exists within some law enforcement agencies. Would a criminal justice professional ever be expected to keep silent about some
illegal act he or she observed being committed by a civilian? No! For a practitioner
to consider keeping quiet about illegal behavior observed in a colleague, therefore,
is baffling and frustrating to those in the profession who are committed to integrity
and the letter of the law.

Ultimately, criminals with bad credentials are discovered—the question is whether
they will be exposed by someone inside or outside of the agency in which they work.
Obviously, an agency's reputation will fare better if the offender is detected and dealt
with internally. Burris (1999) suggests that if police departments create an incentive
for resisting and reporting misconduct, the blue wall of silence can be broken. But perhaps the biggest incentive is the sincerity with which one accepts the mantle seeking
and upholding justice: All criminal justice professionals have a vested interest in cleansing
corruption from their ranks and working in upstanding agencies.

---

[15] To learn more, read the "Police-on-Police Shootings" Task Force Report (2009) commissioned by
the State of New York to identify ways of reducing the prevalence of plainclothes officers of color being
shot by other officers. policeonpolicetf.ny.gov.

The Internet is noteworthy in this discussion because, as invaluable a research tool it is, it can be a double-edged sword. While a virtual necessity for conducting business, the Internet provides plenty of wiggle room for those determined to scam their employers into funding personally consumed goods and services—or to leak information. However, "electronic fingerprints" leave an infinite trail that can be traced forensically and expose misconduct at any time. Being silent about misdeeds does not apply to machines like computers—and it should not apply to you either.

Life Application Exercise #1

Review news stories and popular movies with themes on abuses of power. Evaluate others' actions so that you can assess your thinking on this topic. Did you find yourself focusing on how wrong and negative the villain's behavior? Did you associate negative consequences with him or her, and/or the agency the villain represented? Did you wonder why the offender was not smarter in his choices to avoid detection?

Life Application Exercise #2

Which of these personality characteristics do you believe may be associated with engaging in excessive force—those who bully or "nice people" who do whatever is asked of them?

In my experience, both of these characteristics are personality extremes that are or can be problematic: the bully for obvious reasons and the "go-along" types because they are easily influenced and likely to do whatever the dominants in the group do without question—including maintaining a code of silence.

Life Application Exercise #3

Review a case about public corruption. Identify how the corruption came to the attention of investigating authorities. Did the agency's internal affairs or Office of Inspector General uncover the corruption or was there a tip? Based on the facts of the case should coworkers have known criminality was afoot? Is the agency being criticized for not identifying the misconduct sooner?

Life Application Exercise #4

Romantic "affairs" while distasteful have been the downfall of many professionals, including some working in criminal justice. An FBI agent was reported resigning under pressure after it was disclosed that he had had a romance with the wife of a mobster that he had previously been assigned to protect. (Malinowski, 2003) Pretend that you are a criminal justice employee who has become more and more suspicious about the conduct of a co-worker. The co-worker seems to have developed an intimate personal relationship with an ex-con turned informant. You believe this because the male co-worker and the female informant frequently kid around with each other and are touching more and more in their communications. Next, one night when you are out socially, you run into the co-worker and the informant having drinks together and no work activity is scheduled at the time. A week later, your co-worker attempts to get you to exaggerate the informant's performance to the boss to increase a payment amount. Things deteriorate to the point that all doubt is removed about the nature of your co-worker and the informant's relationship when you catch the informant sharing payment received from the agency with the co-worker. This behavior is regarded as a violation of the standards of conduct for your agency. At what point will you do anything? And what would you do?

There is an old saying when there is damage control after an incident has occurred and blame is assessed, and it goes something like this: "What did you know; when did you know it; and what did you do about it?" And for those situations where there is an issue involving competency, you can assess yourself. There may come a time when you may need to defend your actions. Obviously, hindsight is "20/20" when determining a best course of action is as clear as day. But the important question at the time, with the limited knowledge that you possessed, will be the gauge used to judge your actions. The sooner you perceive there is a requirement for action the sooner you would be expected to act. Failure to act in many ways can be worse than taking actions later determined to have been inferior or advancing a cover up. So commit in advance to acting as soon as possible where necessary—it can save you and your agency.

Life Application Exercise #5

Many who think that minorities engage in crime more than others probably will continue to do so unless they try to resolve this stereotype with a hard look at themselves. However, whereas before this bias could drive a law enforcer's discretionary decision-making, now departments provide behavior-based guidelines that supersede biased and potentially race-based discretionary ones.

Which officer do you believe will have the most difficult time following departmental dictums concerning racial profiling: a.) One who previously, and unconsciously, engaged in the practice—but who now believes it is wrong? Or b.) one who believes that minorities do commit more crime but who does not want to get into trouble, so he vows to focus on behavior before making discretionary stops?[16]

When all is said and done, if unethical behavior becomes ingrained personally or institutionally, corruption ensues. Reinforce your values as needed. If you feel yourself slipping and increasingly tempted to do things you would not have previously considered—seek confidential counseling. Since unethical behavior typically develops in isolation, establishing regular accountability discussions with someone you trust can help keep you on the straight and narrow.

Those walking with integrity should never fear the existence of any organizational screening mechanism designed to get to know you better or an internal affairs unit. Although behaving ethically throughout your career may not make your world perfect, it will surely alleviate unnecessary worry.

---

[16] A good test on racial bias is presented in Burris (1999: pp 209-210). While Burris poses questions which would be good for interviewing police candidates, I think they would also be appropriate for personal soul-searching on this topic.

Chapter 22
A to Z for Building a Solid Career Foundation in Criminal Justice

A — *Anticipate* what is expected of you with respect to your background, both professionally and personally.

B — *Behavioral history*, widely believed to be the best predictor of job performance and ethical standards, is your bridge to the future.

C — *Character* is something you build, not something with which you are born. You can start building your character right now.

D — *Dependability* is key to demonstrating integrity.

E — *Ethics* is everywhere and in every decision you make. Embrace your ethics early and endeavor to engage in ethical decision-making.

F — *Freedom* is the product of behaving ethically, which eliminates the need for lying and the worry associated with it.

G — *Goodness* is something for which you should always strive. Contrary to what many may say, we know intrinsically what is "good." When faced with a choice of personal or professional direction, always choose the path of good.

H — *Help* yourself and others by setting a good example and help them choose the right path.

I — *Integrity* is the measure of who you are and what you do when no one is looking. Strive to always do what is right and do not be surprised if someone *is* looking. Peer within yourself periodically to see if you like what is there.

J — *Just do it.* Self-improvement and character-building are things that you can start at any time. The sooner, the better!

K—*Kill* any tendency or internal/external pressure that pushes you toward making choices that will compromise your integrity.

L— *Learn* from your mistakes and those of others. In developing your own values, study individuals who you believe are of high moral character as well as those you believe are not.

M — *Make it happen.* Only you can act for you.

N — *Nosiness* can be useful if applied discreetly and judiciously in keeping your inner social circle clean and protecting your reputation as well as that of your agency.

O — *Others* can affect your values, integrity, and character—either positively or negatively. Choose your associates wisely.

P — *Pause* to think before speaking or acting. The extra seconds will usually be well spent.

Q — *Query* when in doubt or in the dark about a situation. If you do not know the background or potential pitfalls, ask those who do. It can help you take the best course of action.

R— *Reflect* on the decisions, good and bad, that you have already made. It will help you decide more ethically in the future.

S — *Stop* an action or situation that appears to be going in the wrong direction, before it gets out of control. Never hesitate to put the brakes on a case or course of action when things "go south."

T — *Trouble* may be easy to get into, but hard to get out of. Avoid succumbing to temptations that may lead to it.

U — *Understand* yourself, including your strengths and weaknesses. Work on improving the latter.

V — *Values* are the foundation of your ethical modus operandi. You will see just how valuable your values can be.

W— *Will* yourself to do the right thing. Your will is one hundred percent in your own hands.

X — *"X" marks the crosswalk*. It's a simple rule that goes well beyond the road: Stay between the guidelines both physically on the street and ethically within the criminal justice field, and ensure the safety and survival of yourself and others.

Y—*Yardstick*. While you should regularly take measure of your own character and conduct, they will also be measured by the standards of your agency. Make sure both yardsticks line up ethically.

Z— *Zenith*. Remain focused on achieving the height of career accomplishment. Reaching your zenith is a combination of hard work, a drive to succeed, and strong ethical self-management. Just imagine how comfortable those laurels will be when you can finally rest on them!

Life Application Exercise

Think about what others will say about your character when you retire.

Chapter 23

Conclusion

After considering the standards and examples in this book, you may feel you do not measure up. But you can change your behavior if you are willing to change your thinking, and if you are determined to become a criminal justice professional, these ethical principles should be part of your life. People have said they enter public service in the criminal justice field because they have a strong sense of justice and fairness; consequently, they believe they can do the right thing—and rise to any personal challenge—to facilitate its principles. However, if the majority of the guidelines presented herein have felt utterly foreign and unpalatable to you, changing yourself may not be worth it—and you should consider another field.

From my own standpoint, the driving force of working in the criminal justice field is an ironic one: *I wish to be put out of work.* For this to happen would require that crime no longer exists. It is an unrealistic dream, but one for which so many of us in the profession secretly yearn. How about you?

Concluding Life Application Exercise

Are you doing the right thing for the right reason?
Why do you want to be a criminal justice professional?
Where do your motives originate—from within or outside of yourself?

Examine your answers and assign some weight to your reasons. Are most of your motives based on what you want to do for others, an agency, or for yourself? Are most of your reasons related to you personally or do most of them suggest that you are interested in serving the public? Will you work toward the agency's mission…or are your answers based primarily on what you will receive?

Devoting twenty-five years or more to a line of work is a long time. If your rationale for going into public service is based primarily on benefits you expect to receive versus what you plan to give, think about this some more—and do some preliminary study about public service to understand what may be required. If you are at the application stage, examine the mission statement of your target agency. There is nothing wrong with expecting a reasonable salary, health care, job security, and other benefits; however, if money and power are your main motivations for entering public service, you may find yourself becoming discontent—or worse, corrupt.

You are in the best position to judge who you are, but shaping your evolution is of utmost importance to becoming ethically marketable. Forge onward with head and heart—and best wishes in further solidifying your foundation for success in the criminal justice field.

Appendix A:

Choosy Bosses Choose the Ethically Marketable
By June Werdlow Rogers

Abridged from an article that originally appeared in *opednews.com* published September 10, 2009

It's happened before. The right job has been mismatched with the wrong person. If Bernard Kerik, the former New York City Police Commissioner had become the nation's Homeland Security Secretary, the country's protection would not have been in the best hands. Kerik's personal history was riddled with allegations of criminal behavior—and investigations revealed such a shabby background that he not only withdrew his name from consideration, he was later indicted.

No boss wants to be embarrassed, including the President of the United States. The seven-page pre-employment questionnaire introduced by the Obama Administration in 2008 for candidates is necessarily thorough. Those seeking to occupy cabinet-level positions for the most powerful nation in the world should have no problem filling out a form and be willing to answer in-depth personal questions without fear of what may be revealed about them. If there are no skeletons in the closet, none can be discovered.

This is bigger than embarrassment for a candidate: one vouching for a candidate (like New York City Mayor Rudolph Giuliani did for Kerik), or even the nominating president. America needs assurance that those holding highly responsible positions will do the right thing. "If only we had known" is the wail of those victimized by leaders harboring criminal, tyrannical, dishonest, negligent, or reckless intentions. When the powerful become notorious, a look back often reveals visible flaws of the heart. Finding trustworthy people likely to succeed means going beyond what anyone says about self—it means checking them out.

Since there are relatively few jobs for the many highly qualified candidates, ethics can serve as a filter. All the knowledge and skill in the world in the hands of someone unwilling to do what is right is dangerous. The intense vetting that takes place for every government career employee placed under the wrong leadership can render an agency's mission moot.

Not all failed nominations are "failures." Success occurs on a journey to get the right person when candidates are eliminated because derogatory information bearing on decision-making is identified before hire. Mistakes are different from intentional misdeeds; and every candidate for a sensitive position subject to a background investigation should examine self with an awareness of personal circumstance. Perhaps it is the honor of being selected that deludes some candidates into minimizing past deeds or the likelihood of detection by investigators. But doing what's right is the only ethically marketable guarantee when great opportunities arise.

Even if your prospective boss is not the President of the United States, he or she wants to bet on a winner. The best way an employer can believe you are a sure thing is to dig into your past. It's not being picky—it's being choosy. And choosy bosses choose predictable winners.

Appendix B:

The Most Important Test is Pass/Fail

By June Werdlow Rogers

Abridged from an article that originally appeared in *Self Growth.com* published October 14, 2009

To some, it may have seemed to just be a conversation about a really cute coral colored teddy bear. Honestly, the bear was so striking that it was the first thing I noticed about the guy in the lobby of the military base store who was holding several stuffed animals and had a bag filled with more beside him. The man whom I will call Earl was there to refill a vending machine with prizes.

It was the arcade game with that mechanical claw gizmo a contestant can use to supposedly grab and win a stuffed animal after forking over 25 or 50 cents. Sounds easy, but when I've tried my luck, that claw thing does not seem to have enough umph to pick up anything. Besides, since I have never actually seen anyone win I'm now convinced that Earl couldn't have been there to really make a replenishment (unless it's like the really tiny tellers at the ATM that I just don't see either). I wondered about Earl's real reason for being there. Could it have just been the test?

Just like me, one of the three women congregating near Earl noticed the bear and commented on how cute it was; the other two chimed in their agreement of coral bear's appeal. Then Earl, a military buff who was already trying to solicit sympathy for not being able to shop in the PX, seized his opportunity! "Here, you can have it", Earl earnestly offered. "No thanks," she replied, adding that it would not be right for her to accept the bear under these circumstances. But Earl was undeterred in his determination to force the stuffed animal on the woman. "I saw you just win it" was his next ploy to purchase the woman's soul (okay, I might be a little dramatic here, but are you following me on this?). Again, she declined.

By now, a confused and desperate Earl was offering the teddy to any of the three women, but they all refused, telling him that their positions at the base precluded their acceptance of his gift. No doubt many a woman in the past had readily accepted his tempting offers, but this time he was barking up the wrong tree. A confused Earl was basically begging before the exchange ended. Perhaps Earl was in it to make a love connection and he felt shot down. But Earl would have been out of line even if his inclination was solely romantic; although that was not the only reason he was on thin ice.

Earl's efforts were a clear attempt to ingratiate himself specifically with base personnel, despite the fact that he may not have consciously been aware of this. After all, he didn't offer the adorable bear to the sister sitting nearby who was eyeing it, because he didn't think she could do anything for him. That would be me. And it's a good thing too, because he would have gotten more of the same. As an ethicist I tend to respond firmly on such matters so no one can walk away confused about my integrity. I would have had to tell Earl that he was just plain wrong considering that the stuffed animals were not his private bargaining chips. He brought them there for a purpose and every indication was that they belonged to his company – not him personally – meaning that he could not rightly give them away to anyone; meaning that he failed.

There are no grades in ethics. An ethical test result is either pass or fail. While Earl probably has failed many tests along the way—evident in his tempting offers—those ladies passed with flying colors! I walked up to them and told them how impressed I was. You just never know who is watching.

What's all the big deal? Acceptance of gratuities is the first rung on a descending staircase of corruption. Is anyone who accepts a gratuity going to ruin his or her character? No, but everyone who ultimately becomes corrupt likely enters the gateway accepting small, but improper, gifts.

Would you pass the test even if it was a really cute teddy bear and you had just the right child in mind to give it to? Hopefully, you could resist the temptation, but if you think you would falter, consider this: Would you be comfortable answering questions from the child about the bear's origins? No? Then what—modify the story? See just how slippery the slope is? The right way is the only way.

People face ethical dilemmas every day. Passing these most important tests of all is as simple as making the right choice; and I promise you the more you pass, the easier it gets.

Appendix C:

Don't Eat Crap and Die (the Sobering Facts about Street Drugs)

By June Werdlow Rogers

Abridged from an article originally published by *Self Growth.com*, October 10, 2009

If you looked at a product label and it included ingredients like feces and poison, would you readily ingest it? Well, if you decide to use illegal drugs like cocaine, heroin, methamphetamine, or even marijuana, some nasty and toxic stuff can get into your body. Unlike FDA-approved products with labels, which require professionals to wear white coats, hair nets, and sanitary production environments, street drugs have no such origins. As for the manufacturing sites I saw as a drug agent, two words: hell hole. Here are five nasty, sobering, behind-the-scenes facts about street drugs that you may have never thought about.

Sobering Fact #1: *How do feces and other biological matter get in there?* A common means of smuggling drugs into the United States is to swallow condoms or balloons filled with drugs. Once inside the country, the drugs are pooped out. And trust me, those whose job it is to separate the drugs from the container are most concerned about getting the entire product out above anything else. Easiest way to do that? Cut the latex container—meaning some of the exterior where the fecal and bodily fluid traces are may touch the drugs while being extracted. As the drugs continue their downward distribution, they may be stored temporarily in someone's mouth (hiding place from police) or even stashed by the street runner rectally once again. Of course, this is more than you'd want to know, but consider yourself educated on this point.

Sobering Fact #2: *How do things like rust, lead, mold, or other toxic materials get in there?* Drug traffickers use a variety of conveyances in a subversive way to smuggle drugs into and then across the country. Some of the cargo drums themselves, which may have previously been used to transport other things like gasoline or dirty machinery, can contaminate smuggled drugs. In other cases, the items used as concealment are directly in contact with the drugs. These are things that should never be commingled with products to be consumed, such as furniture, pipes, statutes, tires, shoes, trailer hitches, etc. Once the narcotics are in this country, rogue truckers typically use whatever they are hauling legitimately as cover for the drugs. You name it, and enterprising dealers have probably tried it.

Sobering Fact #3: *How does stuff like baby laxatives, quinine, boric acid, or even rat poisoning get in there?* Well, drug traffickers at all levels want to make as much money as possible, so they are constantly seeking ways to stretch their supplies of the product as filler and buzz enhancers. And if a drug manufacturer, wholesaler, or retailer can represent his product as purer than it really is, he can make top dollar. How is this done? Re-mix the dope and compress it so it's hard and crusty looking—just like the stuff right off the boat.

Sobering Fact #4: *How does the most lethal stuff get in there?* Through various, chemically volatile processes. Methamphetamine straight up is a concoction of harmful substances like red phosphorus, iodine, ammonia, and lithium mixed with cold medicine. But even cocaine, heroin, and ecstasy can contain hazardous materials. Every drug entrepreneur who touches the drug ultimately expands it in some way, even if it's just in the course of re-packaging, so that more money can be made. And that's a lot of touching. Let see: there's the "lab"—somewhere in South America if it's cocaine—that extracts the coca from the plant and converts it to paste; then there's the processing of the paste into powder or whatever form it will take when smuggled (e.g. liquid form, which winds up being transferred by way of clothing saturated with the substance and can mean that dye gets mixed in with it). And then there's additional cutting with any number of substances as it trickles down the wholesale and retail chains. For example, several drug deaths occurring from 2005-2006 were traced to heroin laced with fentanyl (a powerfully strong opiate). Even when a bad batch is discovered on the street, no lot numbers exist for a recall.

Sobering Fact #5: *How did that finger get into the chili?* Somebody put it there, accidentally or on purpose. The pots, pans, glassware, buckets, and other instruments used to make one drug by a given drug entity is often used to make another drug. So sometimes the reason that ecstasy has trace amounts of meth is simply because the manufacturer is using common equipment. Or the reason marijuana leaves have trace amounts of powdered drugs is because of transference when plants are cut with the same knife. At other times, the answer is more sinister and based on greed. When there's "chocolate that got into my peanut butter," it's probably an attempt to get one to love and crave something new. Sometimes traffickers intentionally mix or substitute a more tempting and expensive drug with another, like meth with cocaine, to create a new and more lucrative market. To them, it comes down to dollars: if they can get you hooked on something that will make you come back more frequently, it's more profit.

Consuming crap is just plain nasty and can even be deadly. Drug traffickers' apparent lack of quality control is not usually deliberately meant to be repulsive, harmful, or even to cause death; on the contrary, they want customers coming back for more. To dealers, it's "just business." Just thought you should know what's really being pushed—since no one wants to consciously consume anything that got pulled out of a pile of crap. To those of you who have never used an illegal drug, I say don't try it; you might like it and get to a point where you may no longer care about where the crap came from.

Appendix D:

Use Seized Monies for Treatment
By June Werdlow Rogers

Abridged from an article that originally published by *OpEdNews.com*, August 17, 2009

Imagine this: A person is robbed at an ATM. Police investigate, resulting in the robber's arrest. Meanwhile, money is recovered from the offender. But instead of investigating further if it's the victim's money, police agencies participating in the case split it up. The scenario just described is not that far-fetched when you consider that law enforcement agencies routinely share large sums of money seized from drug traffickers without consideration of the crime victims. How can we take in billions of dollars from drug traffickers annually while permitting their victims to suffer or perish?

Drug dealers are parasites feeding off others without regard to the misery they inflict. Repeat customers whose appetites often result from free samples of addictive drugs deliver high profits to drug traffickers. After being enticed into drug use, many addicts wish they were not enslaved and seek help to stop their destructive behavior. Here's the problem: Research suggests that there are millions of chronic drug users who need but do not receive treatment. While it is debatable how many needing treatment will seek help, less open to question is the demand for treatment in many U.S. cities not currently being met due to limited funding. How can this be?

As a former law enforcement executive, I am ashamed to admit that the answer probably is greed. The stories I could tell you about what goes on behind the scenes relative to determining shared amounts of recovered drug money could turn the stomach. I even read about a local sheriff's election campaign where one candidate boasted about how much better he was at bringing in the drug forfeiture money that his county routinely drew upon. Don't get me wrong—I have no problem with taking every penny of the ill-gotten gains that the law allows from drug traffickers, I just think we need to be mindful of what we do with the money.

First, we need to consider that seizure monies going exclusively to law enforcement may lead to corruption. Rather than doing the right thing for the right reason—namely, drug enforcement—some agencies have reached a point where their efforts are motivated by asset sharing. For example, when I first started working in the drug enforcement field, police departments seemed eager to pool their resources by assigning officers to drug task forces to help tackle the problem. Now, many police departments seem more calculating in delegating officers favoring these assignments throughout multiple task forces. In this way, departments can easily increase the number of revenue streams from which they can share assets regardless of impact on local problems.

Second, we should estimate what effect legislation designating a portion of forfeited drug money to drug treatment would have on ensuring that those who want help can get it. The growing demand for drug treatment because of increased pharmaceutical abuse puts financial stress on our already beleaguered health care system. Consequently, earmarking a percentage of the money seized from drug traffickers to drug treatment seems like a good investment.

Among the many reasons why I have a problem with legalizing drugs is the fact we must never get to a place where we depend on revenue generated that is contrary to the citizenry's well-being. But even with illicit drugs being illegal, if we get to a point like that sheriff where we become dependent upon the proceeds of the drug trade to survive, it is a hard sell that we really want drug abuse to end.

The best possible place for the money to go is to fix the people the drug dealers broke. And besides, I believe my fellow officers would love to do what I had always wished I could do: Get in a dealer's face when you're stripping him of all of his dirty money and tell him that it will be used to help rebuild the lives casually destroyed.

If our federal court system can consider restitution to victims of spam, then we certainly shouldn't have any problem with this one—especially when there is a mechanism whereby we can ensure that the money is funneled through existing programs for drug treatment. The Office of National Drug Control Policy touts the Access to Recovery Program, which bolsters treatment and recovery services. If we really want addicts to be treated, we must be poised to help them at the precise moment they seek it. The way to do it is by convincing lawmakers that recovered drug money should be applied to healing the wounds inflicted by trafficking causes.

References

Associated Press. "More People Find Tax Cheating Acceptable as IRS. Audits Plummet 60 Percent Since 1988," January 21, 2002, http://www.highbeam.com/ (accessed on June 19, 2011).

Associated Press. "9th Circuit Decision Backs Medicinal Marijuana Users," (December 16, 2003).

Barker, T. & Roebuck, J., *An Empirical Typology of Police Corruption*. (Springfield, IL: Charles C. Thomas, 1974).

Bazinet, K. "Air traffic controller suspended, was chatting on phone with girlfriend during Hudson River crash," *The New York Daily News*, August 13, 2009, http://www.nydailynews.com/ (accessed September 5, 2010).

Belluck, P. "Desperate for Prison Guards, Some States Even Rob Cradles." *The New York Times*, April 21, 2001.

Bright, J., *"Clean Dirt," A Memoir of Johnnie Mae Gibson, FBI Special Agent*. (Bloomington, IN: First Books Library, 2003.

Bureau of Justice Statistics, "Background Checks for Firearm Transfers, 2002," September, 2003 (NCJ 200116).

Bureau of Justice Statistics, "11.7 Million Persons Reported Identity Theft Victimization in 2008," December, 2010 (NCJ 231680), http://www.ojp.usdoj.gov/ (accessed May 14, 2011).

Bureau of Justice Statistics, "Law Enforcement Employment Grew Between 2000-2004 According to Justice Department Study," June 2007 (NCJ 212749), http://www.bjs.gov/ (accessed May 16, 2011).

Bureau of Justice Statistics, "Survey of State Criminal History Information Systems, 2001," September, 2003 (NCJ 200343).

Bureau of Justice Statistics, "Traffic Stop Data Collection Policies for State Police, 2001," December, 2001 (NCJ 191158).

Burris, J., *Blue vs. Black: Let's End the Conflict Between Cops and Minorities.* (New York: St. Martin's Press, 1999).

Carlson, D, "Ethics Roll Call," Center for Law Enforcement Ethics, 2003.

City of Ontario v. Quon, et al, United States Supreme Court, 1332 (2010).

Daniel, L., *Federal Personnel Guide.* (Washington, D.C.: Key Communications Group, Inc., 2003).

Delattre, E., *Character and Cops: Ethics in Policing.* (Washington, D.C.: University Press of America, 1989).

"Denied Employment after Background Investigation," *Federal Employees Digest,* November 24, 2003.

Department of Justice, Departmental Ethics Office Webpage, http://www.justice.gov/ (accessed June 19, 2011).

Department of Labor, *Employee Polygraph Protection Act,* September, 1988, (Notice; WH Publication 1462).

Ellin, A, "Guarding Values from the Start," *The New York Times,* June 15, 2003, http://www.contentofourcharacter.org/ (accessed June 19, 2011).

Farrell, G. "Witness in Martha Stewart trail charged with perjury," *USA Today,* May 21, 2004.

Feuer, A. "Drug War Ensnares an Army Colonel Who Fought It," *The New York Times,* April 16, 2000.

Fitzgerald, J. "Drug–Law Activist Axed from Laurel Y Bus–Driving Job," *Billings Gazette,* July 1, 2003.

Friedman, S. (Executive Producer). *The Today Show,* New York, NY: NBC, April 18, 2003, June 2, 2003, and July 17, 2003.

"Gary Johnson wants the government to decriminalize marijuana and tell kids the truth about smoking pot," *The Colbert Report,* May 10, 2010, http//www.Colbertnation.com/ (accessed May 14, 2011).

Gilmartin, K. & Harris, J. "Law Enforcement Ethics...The Continuum of Compromise", *Police Chief Magazine*, January, 1998.

Government Printing Office. "Public Law 109-171," February 8, 2006, http://www.gpo.gov/ (accessed May 16, 2011).

Harris, R. "Unabomber's brother, victim urge bridge between families," *Associated Press*, April 8 1999, http//www.unabombertrial.com/archive/.

Hartley, E. "Lawmakers Target Drugged Drivers," *The Annapolis Capital*, October 31, 2003.

Havill, A., *The Spy Who Stayed Out In The Cold: The Secret Life Of FBI Double Agent Robert Hanssen.* (New York: St. Martin's Press, 2001).

Kellogg, A. "UMass president resigns amidst political pressure," *The Daily Free Press* (The Independent Student Newspaper at Boston University), August 29, 2003.

Lane, C. "A Defeat for Users of Medical Marijuana, State Laws No Defense, Supreme Court Rules," *The Washington Post*, http://www.washingtonpost.com/ (accessed June 11, 2011).

Malinowski, W. & Stanton, M. "Affair nds Agent's Career," *Providence Journal*, November 19, 2003.

Maske, M. "League Issues New Twitter Policy," *The Washington Post*, August 31, 2009, http://www.washingtonpost.com/ (accessed September 5, 2010).

McCoy, K. "High Cost of Bad Cops, City shells out $177 million to settle police misconduct cases." *Daily News*, July 16, 2000.

Mooney, M. & Turner, M. "Students say confessions were coerced," *The Modesto Bee*, July 17, 2004. Posted at http:www.calstate.edu/ (accessed on June 18, 2011).

"Moose wants chance to talk," *American Police Beat*, July, 2003.

Morrison, D. "Some Officers Cash In on Gun Amnesty," *USA Today*, July 28, 2000.

National Institute of Health. *NIH Policy Manual, Official Use of Government Motor Vehicles*, August 15, 2002, http://www1.od.nih.gov/.

"New Jersey Troopers Avoid Prosecution in Racial Profiling Case," *Public Agenda Online*, January 15, 2002.

"New Mexico governor calls for legalizing drugs," *CNN.com*, October 6, 1999.

O'Keefe, E. "Keeping Tabs on the Government." *The Washington Post*, December 4, 2010, http://washingtonpost.com/ (accessed May 20, 2011).

OYEZ, U.S. Supreme Court Multimedia, "*Maryland v. Pringle*, December 15, 2003," http://www.oyez.org/ (accessed June 20, 2011).

"Pentagon Moves to Stop Credit Card Abuse," *The New York Times*, March 28, 2002.

"Report Details FBI Dismissals, Bad Behavior," *Federal Employees News Digest*, March 1, 2004.

Schott, R. "The discovery process and personnel file information - Legal Digest," *The FBI Law Enforcement Bulletin*, November, 2003, http://findarticles.com/ (accessed May 31, 2011).

Singer, B. (Producer). *Access Hollywood*: Court TV, July 12, 2003.

Turner, M. "Misconduct by Professor Found." *The Modesto Bee*, January 25, 2005, ttp://www.modbee.com/ (accessed June 18, 2011).

United States Department of Justice, Office of Justice Programs, Office for Victims of Crime, *New Directions from the Field: Victims' Rights and Services for the 21st Century, Law Enforcement*, 1998.

Yager, J. "Corruption a problem at Customs and Border Protection, agency head says," *The Hill*, June 12, 2011, http://www.thehill.com/ (accessed June 15, 2011).

Zakheim, D. Department of Defense (memorandum), June 27, 2002.